Zai Whitak … is the daugh-ter of the c … ce of India's most famous birdman, the late Salim Ali. A noted environmentalist, she played a major role in setting up the Crocodile Bank and the Irula Cooperative near Madras.

Zai Whitaker lives with her family at the Crocodile Bank in Vadanemmeli near Madras.

ZAI WHITAKER

SNAKEMAN

The Story of a Naturalist

PENGUIN BOOKS

Penguin Books (India) Limited, 72-B, Himalaya House,
23 Kasturba Gandhi Marg, New Delhi 110 001, India
Penguin Books Ltd., Harmondsworth, Middlesex, England
Penguin Books USA Inc., 375 Hudson Street, New York, New York 10014 USA
Penguin Books Australia Ltd., Ringwood, Victoria, Australia
Penguin Books Canada Ltd., 2801 John Street, Markham
Ontario, Canada L3R 1B4
Penguin Books (N.Z.) Ltd., 182-190 Wairau Road, Auckland 10,
New Zealand

First published by the India magazine books, 1989
Published in Penguin Books, 1990

Made and printed in India by Ananda Offset Private Ltd., Calcutta

To S,
who should have lived

The Thalayar Falls are the most prominent landmark as you ascend the ghats up to Kodaikanal. In peak season they are an impressive sight, but deforestation has reduced them to a mere trickle for most of the year.

an explanation

This account, about my husband Rom's work in India, germinated soon after we were married in 1974, at the suggestion of friends. We wrote a couple of reluctant chapters, then gave up; the time was not right, too many ideas were in Rom's head; it would have been a book largely about the possible future. In subsequent years many of these dreams did materialize, as we immersed ourselves in wildlife conservation work.

There have been disappointments as well as much fulfillment. On the whole it has been a decade about which it is a pleasure to write. Proselytising about the conservation of natural resources in a poor country is tricky, but our 'message' has been increasingly about the concrete benefits that wildlife conservation can bring, not just in the long term but in terms of hard, ready cash. This we have demonstrated through the Irula Snake Catcher's Cooperative.

It seemed that the time had come to write the abandoned book. Many young people have been inspired by Rom's work and become actively involved. Others have remained on the periphery and contributed goodwill. Hopefully, this book will make more converts by showing that much can be done without big bucks and a grand infrastructure.

At this time, with our pet project, the Madras Snake Park, in limbo, our own 'success' is the last thing we will take for granted. But for whatever success we may have achieved, substantial credit must go elsewhere. Primarily to both our families, for a steady push onward — to Doris Norden, Earl Whitaker, Gail, Neel, Nina; Laeeq and Zafar Futehally, Murad, Irmela, Shama and Javid.

Shekar Dattatri and Revati Mukherjee have proved the best of friends and partners. The manager of the Crocodile Bank, Harry Andrews, Irula Cooperative staff, Dravidamani and Shyamala and the entire staff of the Croc Bank have played a big part. Harry's dedicated presence has made it possible for us to go away for extended periods and this has been of crucial help. The Dattatri family, and Sandya and Dino Mazumdar have provided an urban refuge for our forays to the city. Govind and Sulochana Swaminathan's personal and professional help is beyond the power of thanks, and Sulochana's tragic death in January '87 has left a dismal gap. Sriram Panchu, our harassed lawyer, has turned into a harassed friend. And gratitude, *rumba nandri* to the Irula, for sharing their jungle lore with us.

My sister Shama Choudhury, took time off from her own writing and two small children to read this manuscript and make detailed suggestions. My parents followed suit, Father even going to the extent of missing a morning's horse ride. Our artist friend Bruce Peck, burned the midnight oil to good effect and we are so grateful for his wonderful illustrations. Thanks to Sharon Westberg for designing the dedication. And last — but perhaps not least — Rom managed to control his impatience with my unceasing questions and prodding, for which I have promised him a copy of this book, duly autographed.

November 1988
Crocodile Bank, Madras

coming home

The Greek freighter, the Hellenic Leader, was an old rust bucket and the slowest ship to grace the ocean. That trip from New York to Bombay in June 1967, she seemed to be chugging away at the same spot, like the Red Queen. She took fifty days getting from New York to the Cape of Good Hope (the war torn Suez Canal was closed) and fifty five to Port Sudan. The food on board was lousy and, even more trying, there wasn't a single pretty girl around. Some relief arrived in Eritrea where, Rom tells me, a teenage beauty threw herself at him while he was innocently walking down the street, looking the other way. So naturally, chivalry demanded a few night revels.

But it was a long trip and Rom, just out of the US Army and on his way to meet his mother in Bombay, must have found it exceedingly tedious; he is not the most patient of people. His mother tells me that at the age of four, he was one of those children for whom special schools were created (to protect normal children) and his teacher at St Lukes, New York City, put up a punching bag for his exclusive use.

For the first six formative years of his life (1943-49) Rom had lived with his mother Doris Norden and sister Gail in Hoosick, upstate New York. During the war years' his father Earl served as a paratrooper and soon after, he and Doris separated. This period at Hoosick saw the beginning of Rom's lifelong fascination for snakes. There were plenty of harmless garters and milk snakes in the surrounding countryside during the summer months, but more important, his mother and Aunt Elly encouraged this hobby and interest in every possible way. His alphabet songs did not follow the usual pattern of A for apple, B for bat; it was A for amphibian, B for brontosaurus, C for coral snake. Doris stoutly defended him when one of his pets, a Dekay's snake, showed up in the glove compartment of a neighbour's car.

In 1951 Doris came to India with her second husband Rama, a Bombay movie man and son of Kamaladevi Chattopadhyaya, one of India's great freedom fighters and later, the main force behind the movement to revive traditional handicrafts. Rom and Gail, aged eight and twelve, were sent to boarding school, at first to Lovedale in the Nilgiris and a year later to Kodaikanal International School in the Palni Hills. There, the evergreen *shola* forests provided plenty of diversion from boring studies and Rom began a systematic collection of snakes, lizards and bugs. Many of these lived under his bed and enjoyed the time and attention that his studies were deprived of. His association with the *sholas* of Kodai spelt the beginning of a deep interest in tropical rain forests and thirty years later he helped form the Palni Hills Conservation Council to protect the unique environment of these hills.

At Kodaikanal, children were encouraged in all outdoor activities and this suited Rom just fine. You could go off camping for the weekend to Gundar Falls, Neptune's Pool, Berijam and other beautiful forested spots within hiking distance. At age twelve Rom made a jump into the world of venomous snakes. A Russell's viper swimming in cold Berijam Lake at 2000 metres up in the Palnis, caught his attention while on a camp. It was carefully picked up in a butterfly net and deposited in his lunch box. It lived with him for a few days, until some of his older friends wisely advised him to get rid of it. By that time they had read in the only snake book in the library that it is "one of the most virulent snakes in all of British India and causes many deaths among natives". And so his first dangerous snake was taken back to the wild and reluctantly released.

But it wasn't long before school kids and outside people started bringing the occasional snake to him, usually the burrowing shield tail snakes, common in the hills, and sometimes the mildly venomous green pit viper locally known as the banana viper. Once a friend's eagerness to bring him a snake ended badly. This friend, Bill Brannen, came back from a hike with a severely swollen and painful hand and related how he had tried to stuff a fat pit viper into his water canteen. It, understandably, turned and bit him on the finger. One of the boy scout friends with him decided to try incising the bite with a hunting knife and this treatment ended up causing more problems than the bite.

Probably the main reason Rom gained a certain dubious notoriety in Kodai was his pet python. Bought from an animal dealer at Crawford Market in Bombay, this two metre snake became a gentle, much handled pet. Technically, of course, no pets were allowed at school. But the python somehow slipped by for several years as part of the empty luggage under the dormitory beds.

Some of the things Rom and his friends did in school makes one wonder how they survived their youth. In the spear and bow and arrow phase they discovered the local blacksmith who turned out superb spear and arrow heads, based on designs copied from Tarzan comics and pictures of American Indians in history books. There were only a couple of casualties during this period. But the fireworks, bomb, rocket phase was to give a few of them burns to remember and some really close calls. They made pipe cannons to shoot marbles way out into the lake, waterproof bombs to blast fish and eventually fairly sophisticated rockets that really went up. They experimented with Molotov cocktails, thanks to Rom's discovery of a little World War II pamphlet *Bomber's Handbook*, and produced everything short of nitroglycerine in the chemistry lab.

During holidays in Bombay, he visited the Bombay Natural History Society to find references on the Palni Hills' snakes and to make contact with professionals. It was here that he first met the ornithologist, Dr Salim Ali and was impressed that an interest in nature could develop into a career. At the Society he learnt about bird collection and skin mounting, which was becoming a favourite activity. In Kodai, fathers at the Sacred Heart College at Shambaganur encouraged him, taught him taxidermy and occasionally let him use their old black powder guns.

When Rom finally graduated from Kodai school he was sixteen and, he felt, not nearly ready for college on the other side of the world. His Indian grandmother, Kamaladevi arranged for him to work as an apprentice with a taxidermist in Mysore. He moved to Vanivilas Mohalla there, learning from and helping V Pradaniah and his sons. They prepared and mounted a wide range of animals, from King cobras to tiger cubs.

The airgun and other school possessions were sold in order to buy a 1941 Triumph motorbike. It was a 350 cc single with mechanical forks and very little spring, but at that age the kidneys are tough. This mobility enabled Rom to travel often to the forests near Gundulpet and Chamarajnagar, at times when there was not much work at the taxidermists. His patron here was Brother Romulus, a jolly Franciscan who was later to start a well known boys' town.

Rom had several jobs at Brother Romulus' farm at Guntapuram. Surrounded by forest, anything that was grown in the fields was quickly devoured by wild boar, deer, porcupine or elephant. He helped keep these animals off the crops with the help of a black labrador and Brother Romulus' two rifles and shotgun, and ended up being the main supplier of fresh meat on the farm. Luckily he never shot an elephant and the one leopard he sat up for, got away. Rather, Rom missed him. But plenty of spotted deer, sambar and blackbuck fell and the gratitude of the farmers always balanced any twinges of remorse.

Those early days of jungle training greatly increased his confidence in the forest. They had numerous encounters with elephants, both by day and night, which gave him the right measure of caution. Meetings with bear, tiger and leopard helped develop a balanced, careful curiosity for the jungle. It was in the forests of Thalavadi and Guntapuram, now almost gone, that he found his first wild python. He was by himself and the snake was too big to tackle. Rom regretfully watched it disappear slowly into the network of caves and crevices that were its home.

In Mysore he started spending as much time at the Mysore Zoo as he did learning taxidermy, and got to know a lot of the animals well. He made friends with a young zoo man from the Hamburg Zoo, Dieter Rinkel, and helped him feed and take care of the seven young elephants that were going back to Germany with him.

Often, knapsack on his back, he would go off for several days into the forests, and unlike most mothers Doris realized the importance of restraining her fears and anxiety. It was probably this one year's total freedom that forever cancelled Rom's wish to sit in a classroom and study.

In 1961 he went back to the States to see his father, and to try his hand at college. It didn't work. He used his brief brush with academics at the University of Wyoming to check out the trout fishing in high mountain streams and to investigate the western rattlesnakes. For the next two years he attempted a variety of careers: he was a truck driver, travelling salesman, unsuccessfully displaying table silverware, ship's messman in the merchant marines, paleontologist's assistant, waiter at a cafe patronized by typists — catcalls at every turn — and lab technician. But the big break came at last. In 1963 he got a job at the Miami Serpentarium, a venom production centre and reptile park owned and run by the legendary snake man, Bill Haast. He produced and sold snake venom for medical research as well as for the production of antivenom serum. For someone interested in snakes it was a fantastic opportunity, working with the most daring and expert snake handler in the world. Many tourists came to see Haast rather than the snakes and were put off by his stony silence and unsociable temperament. They would come and ask the assistants, 'Say, can't he talk or something?'

The other assistant at the Serpentarium was a taciturn snake hunter from South Carolina, Heyward Clamp, who remains a good friend of Rom's. Their day began with cleaning the cages and clearing the compound of various missiles thrown at the reptiles by visitors: tin cans, belt buckles, stricks, stones, cigarette butts. The most challenging enclosure to deal with was that of the four and a half metre Nile crocodile, Cookie. They played at getting him to snap at them and jumping out of reach in time. Fifteen years later Cookie was shot after he killed a child who fell into the enclosure.

The big day at the Serpentarium was Sunday, when Bill Haast took the large Thai King cobras out for venom extraction. He'd spar with the deadly four to five metre snake as it sat up, hood spread in a magnificent defence display. Along the edges of the well tended 'King cobra lawn', cameras clicked on all sides as Haast and the snake watched each other, tense and alert. With knees bent, Haast would close in and jerk his right hand to attract the snake's attention. With a carefully timed move his left hand would flash in to grab the King cobra's neck. There were always gasps as the golden drops of venom trickled down the venom glass. Heyward or Rom would then help him feed the snake with a high protein formula through a feeding gun, which ensured that the snake would both survive and produce high quality venom.

At the time Rom worked for him, Haast had been bitten over a hundred times by venomous snakes and was the only person known to have lived through a King cobra bite. Heyward had been assisting him the day this bite happened. There was a big crowd. When Haast moved his right hand to get the snake's attention, it unexpectedly struck at his left hand which he jerked aside. The irate snake turned to his right hand and caught him off guard; the deadly jaws clamped in with such force that a fang came

Heyward Clamp lowers an eastern diamondback rattlesnake into the snake pit. A diamondback can weigh over fifteen kilograms making it one of the largest venomous snakes in the world.

away with it. While tourists screamed with panic and blood dripped down over his immaculate white shoes, Haast calmly went through with the capture and finished the extraction and force feeding schedules before calling the ambulance.

Haast had not been just lucky with the King cobra bite. He had systematically immunized his system against neurotoxic venoms by injecting himself with increasing doses, until he finally ended up a walking antivenom vial. In fact, his blood was used several times as an antidote to treat people bitten by species of snakes for which there was no antivenom serum. A particularly dramatic instance was in 1966, when a boy in a Peruvian jungle was bitten by a deadly coral snake. At that time there was no antivenom for this species and a severe bite would surely be fatal. The Peruvian government acted quickly. Haast was contacted and arrangements made for his instant departure. The busy highway in front of the Serpentarium, the South Dixie Highway, was closed to traffic. An US Air Force helicopter landed on the pavement and Haast was flown to the nearby Homestead Air Force Base where a fighter jet was warmed up and waiting. He flew to Peru and another chopper took him to the jungle clearing where the boy lay, now close to death. Attending doctors cross matched the blood, found group and type compatible and were able to give the boy a direct transfusion of Haast's blood. Within a few hours he was out of danger and Haast returned to Miami.

In later years Haast further increased his medical fame with his 'venom cocktail', components of which were krait and moccasin venom and which he administered to patients of multiple sclerosis, a paradoxical treatment where venom brings relief.

During Rom's two years at the Serpentarium, most off duty hours were spent looking for snakes with Heyward and other local snake catchers like Attila Beke and Gary Maas, who later became a stunt man in the movies. Then, in the early '60s, Florida's environment was still relatively intact and very different from the endless suburbia of today. Swamp forest which Rom and Heyward diligently hunted was later turned into housing estates and industrial complexes. But at that time they could walk in almost any direction from the outskirts of Miami to get to fairly undisturbed patches of tall flooded grass dotted with hummocks of cypress trees. Hung with airplants and strings of lichen or Spanish moss, they looked like wild, abandoned Christmas trees.

It was a fifteen minute drive to the Everglades on Rom's decrepit BSA 500 single or in Heyward's souped up '61 Ford. In the early winter mornings

The canebrake rattlesnake which nailed Heyward on one snake hunt in South Carolina.

the fog would be low as they walked from hummock to hummock looking for snakes. During the three or four month dry season the water recedes into the canals and forms pools in the hummocks. You could find swarms of water moccasins, watersnakes and fish crowding into pitiful mud holes for coolness. Soon the fish die, their backs out of the water, and this means a feast for snakes, birds, otters, racoons and other predators.

The snake hunts with Miami friends taught Rom invaluable tricks of looking in the right places at the right time. General rules about snakes' habits became the main guidelines. For example, in an area of complete wetness, head for the high and dry spots, and vice versa. Extreme weather conditions like droughts and floods increase the odds of finding snakes tremendously. One evening, Rom and his friends couldn't wait for Hurricane Dora to get over before they started checking the roads. The destruction and high water brought by the big wind had all sorts of creatures on the move, looking for shelter. And best of all, the stormy conditions kept other motorists off the road! Twelve water moccasins and twenty five pigmy rattlers were the venomous snakes caught that night, plus a couple of sackfuls of watersnakes.

One of the local legendary snake catchers of south Florida was Schubert Lee, who shared a house with Rom and Heyward at Coconut Grove, Miami. He caught and sold snakes for a living, often moccasins; water moccasins, the only venomous freshwater snakes in the United States. Schubert knew all the good snake places on the edge of the Great Cypress Swamp with an old canal running along the abandoned Loop Road. They would drive three or four kilometres up the road, get down and look over the canal which was hidden by thorns, tall grass and poison ivy.

Often, they'd see a bunch of harmless watersnakes and among them a couple of black moccasins slipping warily away through the grass and hyacinth. Each of them would have a couple of cotton snake bags tucked in his belt; Rom carried a fairly elegant snake hook fashioned from a golf club and Schubert, the professional, a short stick as they waded into the waist deep, squelchy mud. It was tough going, forging through the warm sludge and thick vegetation, but worth it as almost every few metres they came across a moccasin, often a large one which would sell for four or five dollars.

Sometimes they came upon one at face level and this would be tricky; you had to tread slippery mud while the irate snake vibrated its tail and reared back, mouth open, ready for a strike. It is this spectacular defence display that gives them the name 'cottonmouth' or 'trapjaw'.

One memorable day both Rom and Schubert 'got bit', one after the other. They slithered down to a small ledge and there, behold, were three moccasins about to slip into the water. An opportunity not to be missed by a sane snake catcher. Rom pinned the head of one and bagged him while Schubert started to pull out another by its tail from the tangle of exposed roots on the edge of the canal. You never know where the head might be, and sure enough the snake popped out and bit Schubert on the top of his hand.

'This might mess up our day', was his calm comment as Rom stared numbly at him. They sat down for a smoke on the edge of the canal to wait for the swelling and pain and debated which hospital they'd go to. But there was no reaction; it was a dry bite, with no venom injected, fortunately a very common phenomenon. So back to work.

By noon they were getting deeper into the Everglades hummocks and the loot so far was over forty moccasins. Making a brief stop to curse each other for not having brought food along, they waded now towards the next hummock. Soon after, Rom saw some brightly coloured baby moccasins which were well below the commercial size but would be ideal to rear at home. One had just fed and was fat and healthy looking. Muttering the usual, 'Hang on there, snake', he descended to pin it against the floating log that it was resting on. The log went under, the snake hook slipped and the snake bit him. He lifted it up carefully, dropped it into a snake bag and walked over to Schubert.

'It bit me!' he said weakly.
'They'll do that, sometimes', was Schubert's response.

The pain started soon after and Rom had to sit down as his hand began to throb and swell. They walked back to the car and drove to Miami to ask Haast's advice. He said that though a 'good' bite, it would just be troublesome and that antivenom was not needed. Sleeping was difficult for a few days but soon there were no traces of the bite except that even today the bitten finger becomes numb in cool weather.

That had been one of the last snake hunts with Schubert. One night both Rom and Heyward were out and Schubert was alone at home where they had a collection of exotic and dangerous snakes. A little before midnight, Schubert's girlfriend Florence had a vivid premonition that something

Hunting roadsides and leaves in the Everglades, Schubert and Rom hoped to find the most venomous snake of the southeastern United States, the eastern diamond-back. When spotted they usually curl into a tight defensive coil, rattling ominously.

was very wrong with him, and drove the twenty kilometres to Coconut Grove to see him. She found him lying on the floor, almost totally paralysed. He was still barely conscious, however, able to respond to questions. Florence knew at once that it was a snakebite and asked him if it was a water moccasin. He shook his head. 'Cobra?' Yes, affirmative. He had got one of their big black Pakistani cobras to bite him, repeatedly, on the wrist in a suicide attempt.

Florence was a diminutive woman and Schubert a hefty six footer, but she managed to get him into her station wagon and drive to the nearest hospital. Haast was called and they pumped Schubert with a pint of his blood and 500 ccs of antivenom, but his breathing stopped and after seventy two hours on a respirator, Schubert Lee died. Heyward and Rom, pall bearers at the funeral, were stricken; remorse reinforced grief. They had always known that Schubert had a lot of financial and other problems, but had never attempted to break the barrier of his reticence. If only they had made him talk, if only they'd stayed home that one night or made him come along too. If. They moved out of the Coconut Grove house, haunted now by Schubert's ghost.

Often they would go to the Everglades in the evening after work, since neither Rom nor Heyward was inclined to socialise anyway. Occasionally they were met with the bright red, reflecting eyes of an alligator, which was always a welcome addition to the Serpentarium's collection. One night Heyward spotted a gator which, judging from the gap between its eyes, seemed to be about a metre long. Clamping his headlight on his forehead with the beam directed at the eyes, he picked up his noose at the end of a stick, rope dragging behind, and walked slowly toward his prey.

The gator was on the edge of a large pool, head resting on a grass bank, and dumbly allowed the swivel noose to drop over his head. As Heyward tightened the noose the alligator turned and headed for deep water. He was quite a bit bigger than Heyward had anticipated and Rom watched anxiously as his friend disappeared into deeper and deeper water. Then there was a yell, 'Hey, its big!' and Rom jumped into the water and grabbed the trailing rope. But Heyward had gone under, his hat was afloat and every now and then his head would bob up. Rom knew that alligators were the gentlest of the crocodilians and that Heyward wasn't about to get eaten up. But he was afraid that his friend might have got a hand or a leg tangled in the rope. If this happened the alligator might drag him under the thick weeds. After a struggle, captor and captive made it to the shallows and the struggling animal was trussed up. It turned out to be over two metres long and Heyward, pronouncing himself 'shook', said it was important to 'judge 'them' eyes right.'

Sometimes an animal dealer's interest in a particular snake would take them much farther afield, and Haast would grant a few days leave. Attila was always lucky with old cars and the '55 Plymouth he and Rom rode north in for a rattlesnake hunt was no exception. The Highway Patrol showed considerable interest in the two scruffy snake hunters but always let them go in a hurry when they saw the cargo. They unloaded whatever southern snakes they had with them at an animal dealer's office in New York City. Then they headed inland towards timber rattlesnake country.

They had an order from an animal dealer for fifty big timbers, and Attila was pretty sure he knew where to find them. It was spring. The rattlers, having spent the winter months deep in caves and crevices grouped together in dens, would now begin to emerge, and disperse for the summer.

The rock faced hills around Binghampton, New York was where they ended up. A chat with locals at a roadside tavern gave them a fair idea of where rattlesnakes were seen each year. Leaving the Plymouth, they hiked up through the cedar and poplar trees, flushing grouse and startling a white-tail deer.

Attila's usual canniness brought them to the south face of the rocky slopes and very suddenly, the first rattler appeared. 'Great going, hombre', said Attila as the handsome timber rattler was lifted up and bagged. But then it seemed as if their eyes were playing tricks. In every direction from that spot, there were rattlers basking in the shafts of sunlight filtering down through the trees. They just walked over to the bigger ones and methodically caught and bagged them. Most of them were still close to the den openings in the shale covered slope and some were alert enough to zip back into the safety of their holes.

Rom saw the coil of a fat, black phase timber protruding from under a slab of shale and lifted the rock aside. Beneath was a pile of rattlers several deep and already starting to move. Together, they flipped the big ones out into the open letting the small ones get away — there must have been thirty and more in that pile! A biggy was getting away into a cave so Attila quickly grabbed its tail and was just as quickly nailed by the snake on the top of his hand. He broke into appropriate language and they waited for symptoms. But once more it was a dry bite, and he thanked whoever it is who watches over snake hunters. They got over fifty timber rattlers that day. Rom also caught a few particularly good looking juveniles, to take back to rear at home.

While working for Haast, a hotel owner from what was then Rhodesia offered Rom the manager's job at his small snake park outside of Salisbury. While Rom was preparing to leave, the dreaded 'Greetings from the President' letter arrived. Uncle Sam had got him; it was off to the army for two years, helping in a war he felt bitterly opposed to. He tries to forget the army period, when sadistic corporals kicked you in the backside when you fell, exhausted, before the finish of the mile run, or made you clean less than sparkling shoes with your nose at inspection time.

But there were some good snake hunting days thanks to Uncle Sam, mostly off duty. The two months basic training at Fort Gordon, Georgia in 1965 and then duty at El Paso, Texas, provided an opportunity to see many reptiles he'd not met with before, snakes like the black tailed rattlesnake and the giant Mojave rattler. There were always other soldiers willing to come along on snake hunts... mostly the rabble rousers. Rom remembers, 'One of them, Ponzo, would come back to the barracks at night drunk out of his head and piss on someone, which started a brawl. One night he favoured my friend Jim, and Jim flew at him with a growl and tied him up with the wires of his stereo set. They all went to sleep leaving Ponzo in a peaceful inebriated slumber'.

At El Paso Rom was a lab technician at the army's William Beaumont General Hospital and his work consisted of routine medical tests, not very exciting except the weekly blood sample schedule at Ward 30, the mental ward. He soon got used to wide eyed patients begging him to take more blood, or whacking him as he went by. But these minor disadvantages were offset by the lab facilities and equipment, just right for experiments with snake venoms and for making slides of blood and frozen sections of snake scales and fangs. And every evening it was off to the desert, often the Chihuahan desert across the border in Mexico, looking for snakes, to fulfil orders from animal dealers and venom laboratories on the east coast. The income from this parallel snake catching occupation was useful in boosting the meagre army pay. It was fifty cents for a fence lizard and ten to fifteen dollars for a rattler, depending on the species and size.

It was tricky keeping snakes in the barracks. The wall lockers had to be clear of any suspicious belongings on inspection days. 'Rattlesnakes were a special problem, you didn't want some wise guy reporting strange sounds from Number 133's locker.' In view of this contingency Rom started binding their rattles with scotchtape, and later the captain of the local fire brigade, MK Dick, offered to house his collection. 'MK' and his vivacious wife had a gun repair business and three pretty daughters. Rom visited them whenever he could sneak past the dopey desk sergeant.

One evening he was bitten by a prairie rattler. The pain was a deep, persistent burn and his arm swelled up like a balloon by the time he reported into the emergency room. The team of doctors, happy to have something unusual to do at last, led him off into Intensive Care and started an experiment with Rom's arm in ice for seventy two hours. More painful — and dangerous — than the bite; it was twenty days before he'd recovered from the treatment. Now, twenty years later, the finger periodically swells up and exudes a clear, yellow liquid. The nerves in his finger never did grow back and he hoped that this loss of his trigger finger excluded him from any active war duty.

Rom spent all his leave in Arizona and got to know the beautiful Huachuca and Chiricahua mountains well. Claire, the secretary in the pathology lab, shared his interest in roaming the hills and often went along. They wandered around the shale slopes, often running into coatimundis, deer and bear.

One day's snake hunt took Rom down the Montezuma trail, a steep path leading to Mexico from Miller Peak, at 2800 metres the highest in the Huachucas. It had rained early in the morning and a mist was rising from the ground, ethereally illuminated by the early sun. A movement on the path ahead made him stop short. It was a burly brown bear tearing open a rotten log and noisily devouring beetles, grubs and ant eggs. He must have snuffed an ant up his nose, because he suddenly sneezed loudly and seemed to startle himself. There was only this one route across the steep hillside and Rom had to gently encourage the bear to go away. He flapped his arms and cleared his throat. The bear quickly stopped eating, and looked up suspiciously. Fortunately, he did what was required and ambled uphill away from the path, with one backward glance.

There are over a dozen species of rattlesnakes and numerous other reptilian inhabitants in these mountains of southern Arizona and the periodic ten day leave would fly past like a dream. His most vivid memory though, is of getting bitten by the rare and much sought after green rock rattler.

He was at 2000 metres in the Huachucas before the sun was up, watching coatimundis looking for ripe fruit. Coatis reminded Rom of civet cats back home in India, with their feline features and insatiable curiosity.

One came too close, looked nervously into his face, coughed and they all took off like midget race horses. Picking his way up the old mining trail into Ramsay Canyon, Rom paused to listen to the distant roar of an avalanche. The Huachucas have many unstable cliffs which dramatically collapse to form vast, steep, triangular slides of broken boulders. Perhaps these rumblings were the basis for the Indian name Huachuca, Thunder Mountains. About mid morning, just as the sun was reaching down into the canyon and when snakes would start emerging for an early morning bask, Rom climbed a rock slide, carefully because of loose rock. Suddenly, from under a boulder came the welcome, high-pitched buzz of a green rock rattler. Carefully removing stones around the source of the buzzing, he reached down to shift a large rock. There was a moment's hesitation to find his balance and in that instant a little grey head darted out and caught his thumb. 'Yipes, I'm nailed!' he yelled to the forest. It was a bad bite, a deep two-fanger, and to add insult to injury, the snake disappeared.

Determined to stay away from doctors this time, Rom walked down the canyon to Nell Brown's home. Nell was caretaker for a doctor's country house and apple orchard, and was locally famous for her clairvoyant powers. The house had old, crudely made glass window panes in which she claimed to see future events like accidents, assassinations, marriages, deaths. By the time Rom got to Nell's, a burning, pounding pain was making him moan and swear, and a bloody fluid flowed from the fang punctures. The thumb was a large purplish blob and the hand swollen shiny so that it looked — and felt — like it wanted to split open. Soon an allergic reaction began; twenty sneezes a minute and intense itching all over. This was the first indication of a venom allergy which in later years prevented him from working with venoms altogether.

By mid-day the pain was a lot worse and the evening passed in a sort of semi delirium under the trees in Nell's orchard. She insisted that he sleep in her barn and the good meal, complete with strong coffee that she brought helped enormously. But getting up to click on the light at night, Rom's eyes suddenly went dim. He was clear headed and conscious but totally blind. Losing his equilibrium, he collapsed. He crawled back across the room to his bed and lay down shivering and blinking, afraid to touch his eyes but hoping to somehow blink sight back. It was several long minutes, perhaps ten, before a grey light filtered through.

A few days later he was normal and it was back to business. Venom experts confirmed that though rattlesnakes are pit vipers and so have essentially haemotoxic (blood affecting) venoms, they get more neurotoxic (nerve affecting) as you reach the Mexican border. And this frightening blindness was indeed a neurotoxic symptom.

After six months in El Paso, Rom was sent to Japan to work in US military bases in Honshu, Hokkaido and Kyushu. This was the peak of Vietnam and the young GIs were confronted with the horrifying efficiency of the war machine. Rom was part of the fifteen member mobile blood team of the four hundred and sixth medical lab at Camp Zama and their job was to collect and ship fresh blood to the Nam. This was the first war in which fresh, whole blood was available at the front.

There were all kinds of soldiers. Some couldn't wait to get back and kill, others wet their beds and cried for their mothers in their sleep. Rom became quite immune to hearing the hardened war regulars talk about shooting up a bunch of gooks in the Nam. Camp Zama was filled to overflowing with wounded and convalescing soldiers. There were slot machines at the club and a happy hour at the bar each evening when all drinks were ten cents, and down the road was a skivvy show which featured little stage skits with naked girls of all shapes and sizes.

Six months later it was back to El Paso and the William Beaumont General Hospital. Night duty hours, alone among the long halls of the pathology lab, was a good time for Rom to think about the future, when he stopped being a number and became a person again. Working for someone else, particularly Uncle Sam, was becoming a drag and he didn't have the qualifications to choose his career.

One night, while attending to the blood needs of victims of a local shoot out Rom decided to stake his claim in India. His mother and Rama had separated but Doris continued to live in Bombay with her half Indian children, Neel and Nina. Along with her mother-in-law Kamaladevi, who had become a close friend, she was involved in several projects to revive traditional Indian handicrafts. She was one of the founding members of the Bombay International School, which had been initiated by a group of parents frustrated with the ordinary run of the mill unimaginative schools of Bombay. Neel and Nina, now teenagers, had been among the first students of this pioneering institution.

Rom had last seen Neel and Nina when they were six and eight, and now began to yearn for a reunion with his family. The army years made personal relationships suddenly important, and he tried to work out some way in which he could convert his interest in reptiles into a livelihood in

India. That night of the shoot out brought inspiration. A small venom production unit, he decided, as he assured a frantic doctor that there were two more bottles of A negative in the blood fridge. On his release from the army, Specialist Romulus Whitaker managed to catch five hundred dollars worth of rattlesnakes on a final snake hunt; just enough to buy a ticket on the Hellenic Leader bound for Bombay. He said goodbye to his father, elder sister Gail, who was teaching art at Taft School, Connecticut, and was off.

The Hellenic Leader seemed reluctant to pass up any port without stopping for a day or two. Masawa, Djibouti, Jeddah where the summer heat made strange mirages on the water as the gulls dive-bombed floating garbage in the harbour. Incredibily, it was too hot even to think about going into town with the crew for a taste of African seaport culture. It was nicer in a hammock slung under the canopy at the stern of the anchored ship. A few cans of beer shared with some of the Goan crew, and a fishing line dangling over the side kept the brain from total stagnation.

The ship took another two weeks from Djibouti to Bombay. She had hardly anchored and not yet been cleared by health or customs officials, but Rom managed to jump ship on the pilot boat and get ashore with his rattlesnakes, moccasins and a few personal belongings. Bombay was dirtier and much more crowded than it had been six years ago. But it felt good to lean back in one of the familiar black and yellow taxis and to speak in Hindi with the taxi driver. So much had happened, he'd been through so many important changes, that everything suddenly seemed new and strange. Bombay no longer felt like home base.

Wondering how things would turn out, Rom arrived at Chateau Marine, his grandmother's apartment which had been the familys' home for many years. He took the lift upstairs and everyone screamed in joy and surprise at the unannounced arrival. Half sister and brother, Nina and Neel, had been children in 1961; now they were both good looking teenagers, Nina fair and blond haired and Neel the 'dark sheep of the family', as he called himself! Neel had been playing the guitar for several years and it was obvious he had that special gift which brings an instrument to life. The stack of records Rom had brought was quickly unpacked and the house resounded with the latest Dylan, Zappa and Hendrix sounds. A year later Neel was to form one of Bombay's first 'beat groups', as small rock bands became known there.

The roadside comments as the two-long haired brothers strolled along Marine Drive were, 'Hey, Beatles!' The hippy had not quite come to

India then. But this was 1967 and the hip kids of Bombay were seeing that the West liked Indian clothes and styles. Suddenly flashy shirts and terrycot trousers were out and khadi kurtas and blue jeans 'in'

And along with the music and clothes, the dope scene. Rom had dabbled in peyote and mushrooms while in the army in El Paso. The country medicine shop at the Juarez market just across the Mexican border had an open, ready supply. With Neel and his musician friends he visited the *addas* or dope joints at Churchgate, called *charsigate* by local wits, *charas* being hashish. Here they shared a *chillum* of *ganja* with a cosmopolitan collection of people. A typical group who chipped in fifty paise each for a *goli* of Bombay black, or *ganja*, would be a Bengali diamond cutter, a couple of tough, muscular, handcart pullers, a sprinkling of college students and a taxi driver or two. All over Bombay, these *addas* were the watering holes of the people who preferred to smoke rather than drink, and they had a certain respectability which the local bars didn't. *Ganja* was then sixty five paise for a ten gram envelope at a certain Mohammed Ali Road furniture store. In the army, friends had smoked dried out, weak grass, at ten dollars for the same amount. Obviously, India's freedom about smoking, and the low cost of grass and hash, was a dynamic lure to the flow of younger tourists that was becoming a torrent.

Looking out to sea over the jostling, disorganised traffic from the Chateau Marine balcony, Rom reflected that the post-school years in America had made him soft and used to comforts. The adjustment to the tensions and chaos of poverty-torn India would not be easy. From a distance, coming penniless to India to seek a niche had seemed a romantic adventure. But now he realized it would be a difficult one as well.

the venom centre at gaimukh

As soon as the euphoria of coming home had died down a little, Rom began to plan his venom centre. Venoms from the cobra, krait, Russells viper and saw-scaled viper, the four common dangerous snakes of India, were in great demand in the States at that time primarily for research as significant medical discoveries had been made. Cobra venom was being used to control intractable pain, enzymes in some venoms had been found to kill cancer cells in mice and viper venoms were a source of potent blood clotting factors which were later used to control bleeding in haemophilia and surgery. The project had seemed a cinch, but the initial bureaucratic runaround almost made him give up; he'd been out of India too long, and the reserves of patience and self control needed to face the loops and loops of Indian red tape had dried up. An official in the department of Commerce said that venom export was banned and that Rom would have to get a special licence. But attempts to get one proved futile. 'Why do you want a licence,' the export people asked kindly, 'when there is no ban on venom export?'

Finally the tangle was resolved and a friend, Rajni Zaveri, ran around in the sun with Rom helping him locate equipment for the venom unit. Together they found a beautifully located little house at Gaimukh, on the northern-most point of the island chain which makes up Bombay. It was on the tip of Gorbunder Road which protrudes into the Bassein Creek and the story was that a German biologist had built it before the war. The termites had indulged in a thirty year feast on the doors and windows, and the roof was about to cave in. No electricity and no running water, a well a hundred metres from the house.

When the more vital repairs were accomplished, Rom's girlfriend, Linda Ballou, came out from Miami to join him and they began a quiet life together, looking after the snake collection, writing magazine articles to make a bit of extra money, and doing their shopping on his 250 cc Jawa in Borivli village twelve kilometres away. It must have been lonely sometimes for Linda but she adapted herself admirably to her new rural environment, pulling water from the well and learning Hindi from the local village women. There was a very small village adjacent to the house with a tea shop which serviced the workers from a nearby quarry. Soon the *saamp wallah*, snake man, and Lindabai became popular local figures.

Saturday and Sunday were venom extraction days and Doris would drive out to stand by in the event of a bite, and to take back the venom to store in her freezer at home. At first, snakes were kept in large wooden cages and later in cement pits, round enclosures with smooth walls from which they sometimes escaped. The menagerie usually included fifty cobras, thirty or forty Russells vipers and several hundred saw-scaled vipers which looked like heaps of live spaghetti. Kraits were not easy to come by in that area and Rom would make periodic trips to Madras to buy them from the Irula, tribal snake catchers there who worked for the snake skin industry. He had been introduced to the Irula by Harry Miller, an English photo journalist who had stayed on in India after the war and who worked for the *Indian Express*. These fascinating tribals were later to play a key role in Rom's career in India. Rom also made several visits to the 24 Parganas district in West Bengal to meet the snake catchers of Baruipur. Banded kraits and monocellate cobras were their speciality. During one winter snake hunt, one of the Baruipur catchers found a dozen banded kraits in one termite mound. The same man was bitten on his wrist by a cobra that year. He treated the bite by incising it but in his panic sliced several tendons and in a year his arm was shrivelled and useless. It became obvious that tribal snake catchers were going to be the best teachers of reptile ecology.

At Gaimukh, a lot of Rom's time was spent tramping about in the countryside looking for snakes. Finally, and quite legitimately, he was

West Bengal snake catchers play with banded kraits knowing they rarely bite but aware that they are venomous.

doing what he liked best, although venom orders were few and far between and the financial outlook was bleak. The hillsides behind the house were then covered with forest, the tail end of what is now the Borivli National Park. There was forest across the hundred and fifty metre wide creek too; cultivated areas started only towards Thane, about five kilometres up the road. That was good snake country, paddy fields bordered with thickly vegetated bunds, and Russells vipers were especially common, lurking in cactus hedges waiting for the odd bird or rat.

Identifying the common, widely distributed species was not a problem, Rom had been learning about them since his childhood. But there was no updated comprehensive work on the taxonomy or natural history of Indian snakes; herpetology never was a very popular subject in India. Malcolm Smith's, *Fauna of British India, volume III* was, and remains, the only reference. Smith gives accurate descriptions of the different species but very little about their ecology and habits, and since the book's publication in 1943 there have been no attempts to improve or extend it. This gap was partly filled by studies done by herpetologists in neighbouring countries such as Dr Sherman Minton's report on the reptiles and amphibians of Pakistan, and the late Dr Edward Taylor's classic volumes on the amphibians, snakes and lizards of Thailand.

But it was as much fun delving into old snake books which have now become collectors items, such as Fayrer's *Thanatophidia of India*, 1874, and Frank Russell's *An Account of Indian Serpents on the Coromandel Coast,* 1796. Russell, after whom the Russells viper is named, produced this two volume work, adorned with hand painted colour plates of the common snakes of the area he mainly worked in, coastal Andhra Pradesh. His book's opening words are just as applicable today, nearly two hundred years after its publication, "... the terror occasioned by these numerous reptiles, is immediately aggravated by the indiscriminate apprehension of all being poisonous. To distinguish, therefore, those that are really so, from such (by far the greatest number) as are harmless, becomes a matter next in importance to the discovery of a remedy against their poison".

The remedy — antivenom serum — was discovered and available by the early 1900s. But now in the '60s Rom found at Gaimukh that it didn't reach the poor villager, the most common victim of snakebite, and no effort was made through schools or the media to tell people which snakes to watch out for, or even that an effective treatment existed. His work

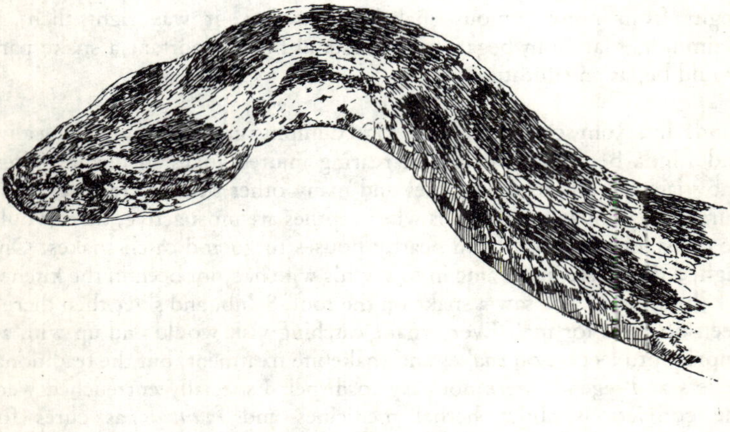

with Dr Yoshio Sawai in 1972 on the subject of snakebite in India highlighted the fact that ninety percent of the fatal cases of snakebite never even got to a hospital and were treated with *mantras* (prayers), herbal preparations and other devices which kept quacks in business.

Since so little literature existed on the subject it was important for Rom to keep in touch with others interested in reptiles. People at the Bombay Natural History Society (BNHS) — J C Daniel, Robert Grubh, Humayun Abdulali and others encouraged him to turn his daily log book notes into occasional papers for the Society's Journal. These became an important part of his book, *Common Indian Snakes*, and the habit of meticulous note taking proved invaluable. The Societys' generous help and active support continues till today.

At the venom centre, orders started to trickle in and Rom and Linda put out the word for large numbers of snakes. At first there was a kind of incredulous silence — then the deluge. Almost every day someone would come galloping down the road, shouting '*saamp, saamp:* snake, snake'. Anything from a worm snake on was called a cobra *(nag saamp)* and every snake was 'as thick as my arm' and 'oh, very poisonous'. People were terrified of every snake; there were reports of deaths from panic and fright from nonvenomous snakebite. In fact, it was right then, at Gaimukh, that Rom began to understand how important a snake park would be, as an education centre.

Linda and Rom soon became the local dumping ground for anything alive and Linda became proficient in rearing injured foxes, fledgeling kites, baby jackals, civets, mongooses and many other smaller creatures. And during the monsoon, which is when reptiles are most active, there would be constant summons from nearby houses to go and catch snakes. One night a desperate man came in to say his wife had not been in the kitchen for three days. 'She saw a snake on the roof, Sahib, and since then there's been no food for me'. Every snake catching visit would end up with an impromptu lecture on snakes and snakebite treatment, but the traditional beliefs and legends were not easy to dispel. Especially entrenched were the convictions about herbal medicines and *mantras* as cures for snakebite, and often Rom had to compromise: 'Okay, take your herbal medicines, but only on the way to hospital!'

One day, a few months after moving to Gaimukh, they were summoned to a nearby field. The villagers had been in the process of uprooting a tree until they came to a snake's tail sticking out of a hole. The inevitable started to pull. It was a large cobra which, like Winnie the Pooh, was firmly stuck. He started to dig with a crowbar and scooped out enough earth so that some of the snake's body was visible. It took a lot more digging and pulling before they were finally able to get him out. A big bulge soon told the story; the snake had eaten a large rat before entering the hole, and suffered for it. But the real culprit of the traffic jam was yet to come. Rom had the cobra in his left hand and was just about to bag it when a large monitor lizard charged out of the hole and ran into the crowd. Some of the men tried to kill it with a crowbar and indeed got the tail, but Rom yelled, 'Wait!' and jumped forward, cobra in hand, to grab it. Soon both animals were safely in Doris' best pillow cases, breathing hard and cursing their luck.

The *dhaman* or rat snake was the most common large terrestrial snake of the Maharashtra countryside and people often called them *nag* or cobra. Rom's diary for 1968 shows that he caught some thirty five *dhamans,* most of them one and a half to two metres long. The largest, two and a half metres, "was in the act of stalking a hare which was crouched motionless, watching the snake, seemingly transfixed with interest or fear — but definitely not hypnotized as it was quick to recognize us as intruders and made off, the snake being detained by means of a leap and a grab". Rom's notes on the *dhaman* continue, "All dhamans are excitable and many bite — somewhat clumsily at first — but most will become tame if handled regularly. Six of those caught emitted a fairly loud 'growl' from deep in the throat when grabbed. When approached in a corner or cage they will expand their throat, arch the neck and body and make rather spastic lunges with partly open mouth. When encountered in thick bushes they often get away, having the advantage in thorny and rocky places. They may be captured by either jumping on them before they get away, although their superficial resemblance to cobras makes this a dubious practice, or a helper could try to head the snake off and drive it towards you. I have also dug them out of rat tunnels, from under the roots of trees, from rock piles, rubbish and from out of the hollows of trees. Colour variation from deep olive-almost black-to very light brown and the young in the area are a 'medium' greenish brown. Most specimens feed well in captivity even taking long-dead rats which they kill by pressure from body and mouth rather than by constriction; frogs swallowed alive, sometimes beeping in protest all the way down into the snake's gut. On July 13, a 1.8 metre female laid 14 eggs, 13 hatched on September 16th and 17th; average length of hatchlings 285 mm."

Being called to catch a snake or monitor, the latter often considered poisonous, was always exciting and educative and brought Rom closer to the rural Indian with whom he has a natural affinity. But summons to treat snakebite victims were mostly grim; hospital and antivenom serum was always a last resort and several of the patients brought to him were too far gone to help. However, sometimes seemingly hopeless cases came round with antivenom, such as a fourteen year old boy bitten by a krait and carried in totally paralyzed. There was no time to get the doctor and Rom gave him two ampoules of antivenom intravenously. The boy recovered in an hour.

Apart from extracting and selling venom, Rom was also collecting snakes for Haffkine Institute, then as now a major producer of antivenom serum in India. He went on several snake buying exercises on Haffkine's behalf to other parts of the country and one of these took him to Ratnagiri district, south of Bombay. Here, saw-scaled vipers are common during the rains, then disappear like magic for the rest of the year. More hazardous than catching these vipers is the overnight bus journey from Bombay to the small town of Deogadh. The bus swings along the steep ghats like a roller coaster and Rom noted anxiously that the steering wheel spun like a top and the gear box was held together with rope. When it was time to change gears, the gallant bus conductor leaped on to the gear box and tugged away with the driver.

Anyway, in spite of this team effort or perhaps because of it, the bus did get to Deogadh. The Ratnagiri landscape is spectacular, red laterite tableland with steep cliffs plunging into the Arabian Sea and small patches of jungle dotting the stark expanse. But the moonscape tableland is the most prevalent and the boulders scattered all over provide ideal habitat for the saw-scaled viper. Its prey, mice and scorpions, are correspondingly abundant.

A local tribe, the Mahrs, are the traditional snake catchers in this area and Rom contacted them through a merchant friend, Mr. Doshi. They agreed to take him along on their *phoorsi,* viper, hunts over the next few days.

It rained every day, some days without ceasing, on others in short dynamic cloudbursts. The air was always hazy with moisture, the rocks always slippery. The twenty Mahrs and Rom split up into groups of two or three, and each had four basic pieces of equipment; an umbrella, a pair of tongs, a stone turner and a snake container. The Mahr stone turner was a short, bamboo pole with a long iron spike at the end; the tongs were improvised with strips of bamboo bound about ten centimetres up one end, forming a metre long pincer clamp. The container for the *phoorsis* was a cowdung plastered conical basket with a weighted coconut shell cover.

Rom and his two Mahr companions would start early, walking fast and covering fifteen to eighteen kilometres, occasionally coming across the other catchers. It took Rom a couple of days to learn the art of walking on the slippery terrain without falling every few steps (with a clatter of umbrella and snake hook), at which there was a healthy roar of joy from his friends. Barefoot was best but he didn't have the leathery soles of the others and suffered. Their job was simply to walk through the great fields of boulders, turning over every likely rock. They averaged about a hundred rocks turned for each snake — but sometimes Rom would see veteran catcher Jamsandekar in the distance, huddled under his umbrella, stooping and straightening, bending and unbending with a snake almost every time.

One afternoon they walked south along the rugged coastline, crossing the many creeks and skirting the cliff edges. The surf boomed below and the air was thick with humidity; walking was like treading water. They headed inland towards Lindahl and began the zigzag walk that would take them back to Deogadh, turning over rocks as they went along. A family of jungle crows followed them for a long time, cleaning up the crabs, scorpions, earwigs, earthworms and chameleons that scrambled out as their homes suddenly vanished. After a while Jamsandekar's loud laugh rang out.

'They are good snake hunters', he shouted, pointing to the crows, which were now turning over the smaller stones themselves. That night after a bath, Rom lay back in one of the long armed resthouse chairs, watching the rains sweep down in sheets. It was pitch dark when a man came tearing in holding a kerosene lamp, soaked and panting. '*Saamp*, Sahib, *saamp!*' 'Where?'. He said there was a big cobra in Mr Doshi's house, so Rom jogged the wet kilometre to the village and through a crowd in front of the house. Several men had long poles, one had a double barrelled shot gun. Everyone gave an account of how the snake had come in to the house out of the hard rain, crawling right past several people and ended up in a storage bin. 'It's as thick as my arm', said poor Mrs Doshi, but her neighbour corrected her. 'No, it's as thick as my leg'. And sure enough it was a good sized cobra, one and a half metres long, full of beans and furious when Rom hauled him out of his comfortable dark bin.

The next evening there was a repeat performance, only this time it was a Russell's viper in Mr Doshi's secretary's house. This sort of open visitation by snakes was not that common; but it had rained exceptionally heavily on both days, and snakes were seeking dry refuge after being flooded out of their holes. By the end of the week Rom had two thousand of the small but deadly saw-scaled vipers carefully packed for the trip back to Bombay.

Soon after, Rom and Linda went with Harry Miller to Battis Shirala near Sangli, Maharashtra. Harry was at that time writing an article for the *National Geographic* on cobras and so was gathering information on cobra worship during the harvest festival of *Nag Panchmi*. In Battis Shirala the festival is celebrated by worshipping cobras caught in the wild with their fangs intact, unlike most places where defanged cobras are used. The local people here believe that many years ago a guru granted them immunity from snakebite. Farmer, labourer and merchant set out to catch cobras a few days before the festival. Snakes are kept in mud pots and released back into the fields after the celebrations are over.

Harry, Rom and Linda arrived at the small town to see processions of bullock carts with raised platforms; on these sat men with one or more cobras. Intrigued, Rom asked to examine the snakes and gently prised open their mouths to find the fangs intact. There were people walking down the street with a rat snake or racer round their necks, children shuffling along draped with two or three banded racers or rat snakes.

In the evening, the cobras were arranged on the pavement and entertained with small pots half filled with pebbles, which a charmer shook back and forth. There were white spots on the bottom and this combination of the startling spots and the pebbles' vibrations made the snakes spread their hoods and sit up; the defence display universally called the cobra 'dance'. Apparently, these tricks of the trade had been passed on to the people by the guru, along with the immunity to snakebite. Monitor lizards also played a part in the festivities and hundreds of them were trussed to poles and marched up and down like some bizarre parody of a crucifixion.

When there was a lull in the procession or time out for a tea break, the monitors were stacked against a wall like many broomsticks. At the end of the day the cobras were brought to a central area, where there were tens of thousands of people and the shouting and revelling made a permanent roar. Finally, over two hundred cobras were lined up, hoods spread in a sort of swaying inspection parade, and women stepped forward to worship them with ghee, red *kum-kum* powder and flowers.

A large venom order was just coming through from the United States when the Government banned its export, this time for real. Since the indigenous market consisted of known institutions like Haffkine that produced their own venom as a policy matter, it was the end of the road for the venom centre. Rom was bitterly disappointed. The venom centre had seemed the perfect job for a herpetologist. Now he was back at square one and felt that a year's effort had gone down the drain. He also needed a physical change of scene, and decided to move to the epicentre of snake hunting activity, Tamil Nadu, in a sense his home state where Kodai school is located. For someone who had failed to find like-minded friends, here was a goldmine: a community of over a thousand Irula tribals doing nothing but catching snakes. He'd already been organising consignments of snakes from the Irula to Haffkine.

He and Linda found a small house on Chamiers Road in Madras for four hundred rupees a month, with plenty of storage space for crates of cobras, vipers, kraits. They only had to make sure the landlord didn't find out what they were up to.

the madras snake park

'Thirty kraits, fifteen cobras, five Russells vipers, *Suratai pambu?* Let's see... two, four, six, eight'. Like a dhobi counting clothes to be washed, Arjun and the other Irula totalled up their catch for Rom. He was on one of his periodic visits to their village on the outskirts of Madras on his Jawa motorbike, to buy and take away the snakes they'd caught for the Haffkine Institute. Ten rupees per cobra, fifteen for a krait or Russells viper. Saw-scaled vipers came wholesale, in bunches, fifty paise per snake. Fortnightly consignments were sent to Haffkine in Bombay, in thin, muslin bags which a local tailor was kept busy making. In fact, he'd become a professional snake bag maker. 'Sixty krait bags', would be the order, and he knew exactly which type of cloth to use, and what size they should be. He'd run his sewing machine up and down the seams in a frenzy, determined that no snake should ever escape from his bags. Apart from the danger of their escaping, species such as the krait had to be carefully packed since they are cannibalistic, and a group could be much reduced by the time they got to Bombay!

With this deadly cargo strapped to the pillion of his bike, Rom would sputter to Central Station and book it on the Bombay-bound Dadar Express. At first the railway officials were horrified and understandably reluctant to have anything to do with the knobbly boxes, with their sinister skull and crossbones signs. 'I am sorry, but we cannot accept. We cannot book. It is beyond scope of Indian railways'.

'That's nonsense!' replied Rom, and very nearly terminated his career right there. The official was furious. 'Nonsense! You are calling me nonsense! Okay, let us see ...', and so on. Soon people appeared from all sides to participate, encourage, discourage, threaten. But somehow after ten minutes of wrangling it was sorted out, and as happens so often in the sudden, heated flare-ups of India, everyone parted on excellent terms. There was never any problem after that, and the kraits, cobras and vipers chugged to Bombay in comfort.

One of the first Irula tribesmen that Rom met in Madras, and who later became a close friend, was Natesan, a tall, spry, sharp featured snake hunter with shoulder length hair. Together they roamed the rocky scrub hills of Chinglepet district, learning about the reptilian creatures that live in these rich habitats. Rom soon found that Natesan could answer all his questions about the snakes of this area which the academics and local naturalists were unable to do. His Tamil improved under Natesan's exacting tutorship, and the Irula invented an English of his own, mostly a combination of swear words and hip jargon. His favourite expression was 'Sure, man!' and Sureman was what he came to be called. As they drove out on the motorbike and covered several miles on their quest for snakes, Natesan pointed out medicinal plants, described the monitor lizard's breeding habits and more, a Pandora's box of natural history information that Rom was extremely privileged to share with him.

Soon after Rom and Linda arrived in Madras, Natesan took Rom out for a weekend in the Guduvanchery area. This was the mating season of the spectacled cobra in the south and a week earlier Natesan had seen two females and seven males in one hole. A bonanza for a snake catcher! It was a crisp, clear, cloudless and eventually very hot day as they walked out into the scrub jungle, Natesan bare bodied except for a *veshti* and carrying a crowbar, Rom in jeans and no shirt. Within ten minutes, Natesan had found his first cobra. He'd seen a faint scrape on the ground, on a bund that separated two rice fields, and followed the track through a patch of scrub to a rat hole ten metres away. It was very fresh, he said, and it was a cobra. 'How do you know?' asked Rom. 'From the track'.

Natesan started digging. It was the hole of a *vellai yelli,* a gerbil, which he deduced from the hair and droppings as he dug on and on. Every now

The monocled cobra of northeast India appears to have a weaker venom than the more familiar spectacled cobra. It seems to be more aquatic than other cobras and commonly eats fish and frogs.

and then he would stop to examine the almost invisible signs in the mud, and to work out which way the tunnel turned. He then walked over to a shrub and snapped off a fresh, green twig. Natesan pushed it into the winding tunnel, but there was no movement. A little more digging and the twig was inserted once again, and this time it gave a convulsive jerk; the cobra was at home! He now stopped the horizontal digging and tackled the roof of the burrow. Two or three powerful strokes of the crowbar and there it was, wild and beautiful, striking out with all the energy and verve of a cornered animal. 'He is a big person', murmured Natesan, as he side-stepped to avoid the snake's strikes and Rom opened out a snake bag. Using a stick, Natesan held the tail and lifted the snake gently into the bag, which Rom quickly knotted.

A freshly caught cobra is very different from the sick, defanged ones that travel in the snake charmer's basket. But even when first caught, few will actually attack with an intention to bite. Most strike with closed mouth and make every effort to get away. The Russells viper on the other hand is another story, leaping up, sometimes with most of the body off the ground and striking repeatedly when in danger. During a survey of the reptiles of Pudukottai for the Tamil Nadu archives, Rom found that this district, formerly a princely state, was Russells viper paradise. In two days he found no fewer than thirty of these deadly snakes.

After bagging the cobra, Natesan stopped to wash at a small pool of muddy water and saw a yellow head sticking out of a crab hole on the bank. Soon he was in waist deep water with a struggling, checkered keelback watersnake held firmly in one hand while he checked the other holes for more. Later, as it began to cool down, a chocolate streak zipped by on a nearby tamarind tree. 'I'll shake this person down, be sure to catch him as he falls', shouted Natesan, clambering up the tree trunk. He shook the lower branch it was resting on, and soon the snake sailed gracefully down and into Rom's arms. They continued on their way, through the groups of pre-historic dolmens and ancient burial sites which lie scattered around the countryside outside Madras.

Learning snake hunting techniques from their fathers as soon as they can walk, many of the Irula have a kind of third eye for snakes, and seasonal micro-habitats of various species are pinpointed with amazing accuracy. The ubiquitous land snakes like the cobra, krait, Russells viper and the saw-scaled viper, the 'Big Four', are perhaps the only species that have benefitted so completely from the large scale conversion of forests to agricultural lands in recent years, and it is typically in scrub or in cactus hedges bordering fields that they are most abundant. The alternative, seasonal habitats remain: kraits in their brick and rubble piles, cobras in thick, evergreen scrub forest, Russells vipers in cactus hedges and saw-scaled vipers in open, rocky places. But it is the rice field, with its abundance of rodents and plentiful supply of fresh water, that has become the refuge of the commoner species.

Snake hunting with the Irula was fantastic. But sending consignments to Haffkine was on the whole a sweaty, underpaid job and Rom felt he deserved a better fate than weaving in and out of traffic with crates of snakes, especially after one bad fall with bags of cobras flying in all directions. He began thinking seriously about setting up a snake park which would teach people about snakes and snakebite, and also campaign for the conservation of reptiles. Sureman lit a *beedie* and peered through thick, matted hair as Rom explained his idea of a 'snake park'. He cocked his head to one side questioningly and rubbed thumb and forefinger together to make the sign for money. 'Visitors', said Rom, and Natesan threw back his head and laughed till the betel nut juice bubbled at the sides of his mouth.

More and more, it seemed the right thing to do; countering the wealth of myths and legends about snakes in urban and rural India with hard facts would help people as well as snakes: it would reduce deaths from snakebite, and stop people from needlessly killing all snakes. It wouldn't take much to prove to people that conserving rat-eating snakes saves their fields from the depredations of rodents. A small education and conservation centre for reptiles, Rom decided, tying on his last consignment of wriggling cargo. It would mean investing at least a few thousand rupees, which is a lot of money when you don't have it. He often thought wistfully of that one thousand dollar salary he had earned as a twenty year old merchant seaman and wondered why he hadn't saved any of it. But at that time it seemed a ridiculous thing to do.

So he took the plunge, and became a reptile missionary. 'Third time lucky', encouraged Neel, referring to the two previous adventures in trying to make a living through snakes in India. It had been an exciting but also intensely frustrating period and Rom knew that if this project didn't succeed he would have to go back to the States to get a job. He made up his mind to give it all he had.

This was '69, two years after his return to India and the only assets left were two good camera lenses and a pile of gramophone records, which he sold to raise money for the new project. Good luck and coincidence came to the rescue at this critical stage, including a small cottage with an acre of land advertised for rent near Selaiyur village on the Velachery road. It was a forty five minute drive from Madras city. The rent was only a hundred rupees per month but even more incredible, there was an unfinished house foundation in the compound which provided nine readymade snake pits. Rom and Linda grabbed it and Neel and Nina came from Bombay to stay with them and help in the crucial initial stages.

The first big job was to clear the debris away from the foundation and armies of local village children arrived every morning to work. They soon learnt that employment did not necessarily mean instant pay, but worked hard and willingly anyway, and finally Rom had to pawn his last possession of any value, a gold chain, to pay their wages. Rom applied to Citibank for a loan of ten thousand rupees and much to his amazement, got it. With this money, the inside walls of the pits were plastered smooth to prevent snakes from getting out and a few signboards made about snakes which were carefully removed every night, being the only assets of the park besides the snakes. There were very few visitors that each got a lion's share of attention from the staff. In fact, every time someone came in, a holler went up, from entrance gate to pit I, and so round the park, until all four or five attendants were in readiness to receive and educate the tourist soundly. There were rehearsed speeches in Tamil and English about identifying what Rom dubbed the Big Four dangerous snakes, the treatment of snakebite and a little on the natural history of snakes. And when the tired visitor finally wiped his brow and headed towards freedom he was told-and reminded-never to buy snakeskin wallets and belts or allow his friends to do so.

Selaiyur was too far from the city for the park to make money — the twenty five paise tickets rarely covered salaries and maintenance costs — but it certainly did become well known, and very quickly. The long haired American hippy who lived with snakes and swore in Tamil was a natural target for the press and I, then in tenth grade at the Bombay International School, remember seeing several strange headlines in newspapers and magazines about him and his snake park: "Hippy adores snakes", "Plucky American starts venomous venture", and so forth.

World Wildlife Fund-India, which my sister Shama had got off the ground after half a year of working at the International Union for Conservation of Nature in Morges, Switzerland, was then in its infancy, but gave the Snake Park a vital donation of five thousand rupees; and that was how Rom first appeared on my horizon. My father, Zafar Futehally, was the honorary secretary of this organisation as well as of the Bombay Natural History Society and Shama, studying for her BA at St. Xaviers

College, worked with him whenever she had the time. Together, and then with very limited resources, they managed to get an organisation going that was to be the core of the big conservation movement of the 70s. I helped Shama in the office. Our newsletter, produced four times a year for WWF members, was becoming widely read. One of its earliest contributions was an article on Silent Valley by one Romulus Whitaker from Madras. Along with it came a request, five thousand rupees for his reptile research and conservation centre.

Soon after, Rom came to Bombay to meet my father and collect his grant. I remember Father coming home very amused that evening, and very taken with the 'snake fellow'. Apparently, while they were both on their way out of the BNHS office at Hornbill House Rom said, 'Uh Zafar, could you lend me fifty rupees?' My father took out his wallet and gave him a note. A few steps ahead, Rom turned magnanimously to him and invited him to lunch. How we roared over the story.

Rom became the Southern Regional Representative for WWF and for the next seven or eight years the Snake Park was the headquarters of the organization in the south. As a fund raising unit WWF Madras was a total failure, but in the sphere of educating children about wildlife and conservation it made a marked contribution right from the beginning, through talks at schools and colleges, the now famous snake shows and organized outings. Rom publicized WWF by wearing a large panda badge on his lab coat and word spread in the village that he was a policeman for bears and snakes.

He was away often, hunting snakes with the Irula tribals or visiting the high rainfall forest areas in the Western Ghats. Nilambur valley, at the foothills of the Nilgiris, was a favourite haunt and a series of camps in Silent Valley, Kerala, helped lay the foundation of what was to become the biggest environmental battle fought — and won — on the sub continent. Naturalist friends such as David Hayles and entomologist Chris Pruett often stayed at the Park to help with the increasing work load, typing, filing, buying snakes, showing visitors around as needed.

There was often a crisis when Rom was away; that was when things went wrong if they were about to. One evening an ascending premonsoon thunderhead blocked out the sun and the sky exploded with thunder and lighting. The rain swept in and continued for several hours, swirling and crashing over south Madras. Fortunately, Rom's brother Neel decided to check the snake pits. A partial palm leaf roof prevented the snakes from being flooded out but a fallen branch or pole could easily have provided

Deep, still waters of the Kundipuzha River in Silent Valley.

an escape route and they always seemed to be stimulated to unwanted activity during heavy rains.

Huddled in a torn, plastic raincoat Neel checked the cobras with a wavering torch beam. All okay, a few crawling around in the enclosure while the others lay in heaps at the corners. Kraits and Russells vipers similarly occupied. 'But man, I freaked out when I saw the *suratais,*' he recalls. Swimming joyfully up the wet walls were twenty or thirty saw-scaled vipers, thin and light enough to adhere to the smooth, soaked wall. Some had made it to the top and three were crawling around in the wet mud inches from Neel's bare feet. He began searching for the ones which had actually got out of the pit and flipped them back with a snake hook. Then he scraped the eager wall climbers back in only to find they promptly crawled up again. He knocked them down repeatedly, but they seemed to think it was some kind of game, and it only spurred them on. There was only one thing to do; transfer them to a closed container, so he charged back to the house in the rain and returned with an empty two hundred litre drum. Just right for truant vipers. Nina joined him and the two somewhat unwilling snake keepers spent the next hour rounding up over a hundred saw-scaled vipers.

As at Gaimukh, victims of snakebite from adjoining villages came to the Snake Park; even in the unlikely event that antivenom serum was sought soon after the bite, the hospital was thirty kilometres away, taxis were not to be had, buses were infrequent and the last one left the village at 9.30 pm. These logistics often made a farce of the message about antivenom serum. But there have been several lives saved by innovative travel to hospital by bullock carts, stretchers and bicycles.

Some victims came in a state of shock — eyes rolled back and foaming at the mouth — from the bite of a harmless watersnake or rat snake, and the only treatment necessary was a smart slap and a sound scolding, with perhaps an aspirin for good measure. More often though, it was a serious bite, usually from a krait. The classic krait bite in rural India happens when the person is sleeping outside his hut at night, on the ground. Flicking in their sleep at a krait out hunting for rats and mice, they are bitten and often die hours later without quite knowing what had happened. The definite, dramatic, paralysing symptoms of krait bite are often apparent only at the end, when there is not enough time to get to hopsital. One morning at 5 am, Rom was woken by a farmer whose daughter had felt something bite her in the night and who, he said, had fainted. 'It is not serious, some tablets will set her right', he said, adding that she was of a very nervous disposition and even a bee sting could send her into a faint. His confidence made Rom's subsequent task doubly difficult; they sped back to his farm on the motorbike and peering into the dark room Rom saw that she was dead. Kraits are insidious killers indeed, and the legend that they suck your breath away while you sleep is not very far from the truth.

At that time most Irula scorned hospitals and antivenom serum, placing implicit trust in their own herbal remedies such as *veley yerege*, a mixture made from pulverized bark and herbs. Chockalingam, an Irula snake catcher, is widely known for his herbal treatments of snakebite and has himself survived ten cobra bites. But having seen antivenom at work, he concedes that his treatment may have a lot to do with the high percentage of non fatal, non serious bites. His medicine for saw-scaled viper bite is very interesting and merits detailed medical examination, since he has used it for several serious bites with unfailing success. This statement may sound heretical to the scientific community, but the fact remains that the Irula are scientists in their own right and their medicines are not to be confused with those of the ubiquitous village quack. At the present time, Chockalingam is in the process of 'immunizing' his son, Kali against saw-scaled viper venom, giving him a swallow of a herbal mixture once every month on the day before the dark of the moon, for six months. His older son Rajendran, also immunised, has been bitten badly by saw-scaled vipers three times, and is none the worse for it.

Natesan was one of the hard liners who swore he'd never take antivenom serum. He often argued about it with Rom in the strange English he'd absorbed. 'Hey man — I had so many bites and no problem, so why I waste money on those silly cardboard boxes?' His confidence almost killed him though when he celebrated a neighbour's wedding rather too gamely and as tight as an owl, began to demonstrate his snake handling prowess. He brought out a cobra, got on his bicycle and took the snake for a ride on the handlebar. For a few seconds everything was fine-cheers and claps from the audience — then the thoroughly frightened snake bit him hard on the thumb. By the time he came to Rom's house he'd taken large doses of the *nava Kunji* herb he swore by but the first symptoms of paralysis had set in. His eyelids drooped heavily, his speech was slurred, and breathing difficult.

As a non medical man it was illegal for Rom to give him antivenom but there was no way he could get him to a doctor in time. There was as usual a stock of antivenom in the house, and Nina boiled a syringe in deathlike silence as they wondered if it wasn't too late to save old Sureman. The tourniquet above the bite was gradually loosened and so after the 20 ccs of antivenom serum began to course through his veins, Natesan sat up and grinned foolishly, reeking of his celebrations. 'I'll stay away from cobras for a while', he mumbled. 'How about staying off the other poison instead?' But Rom's suggestion was not taken seriously and Natesan died a few years later, of multiple liver complications.

Natesan's death was like the passing away of yet another era. Despite the vast cross cultural gap they had become close friends, brought together by their mutual fascination for the jungle. Sureman had been with Rom to every major forest in south India, collecting interesting species of snakes for the Snake Park. He was also an excellent showman. Tourists loved him and he became a widely photographed Irula. But the one thing Rom could not influence him about was booze, and he watched his friend's mental and physical deterioration helplessly.

The continuing contact with snakebite and the issues of public education about antivenom serum and its adequate distribution generated a symposium jointly by the Snake Park and the Madras Pharmacalogical Association in 1977, which was attended by doctors and paramedics from many parts of the country. But despite these efforts, the health authorities have done next to nothing to reduce the ten thousand snakebite deaths every year.

In 1971 the Tamil Nadu Forest Department agreed to lease Rom an acre of land in the beautiful Guindy Deer Sanctuary. The Park's move to this central location was a vital step in its growth in every way; from then on, there was no looking back, except perhaps to the peace and calm of preceding years. The move was easy, since there was not much to move, and in a short time the Madras Snake Park became a famous touristic alternative to temples, with over a million visitors a year and regular coverage in the press. A year after the shift to Guindy, Rom formed a Trust with seven members to run it. Unfortunately serious differences arose among the Trustees in later years, and Rom decided to walk away from his brainchild in '84. It was not easy to say goodbye to the carefully reared reptiles, the invaluable reprint and library collection and the many old friends.

The Irula snake catchers, backbone of the Park since its inception, complained of the long bus ride into town with their muslin bags bursting with snakes but this was the only drawback of the Guindy location. The early 70s were teething years and much money and time was wasted designing, building, demolishing and re-building reptile exhibits which would both suit the hot Madras climate as well as satisfy the visitors curiosity.

Rom's frequent jungle trips were teaching him about reptile requirements in their natural habitats and he was transferring this knowledge to the park. An awareness of a reptile's temperature and humidity needs, in other words the micro-climate that it is dependent on, was the main key to keeping them alive and healthy. For example, observing pit vipers drinking the rain water dropping on their rough heads and saw-scaled vipers collecting tiny morning dew drops for their thirst, taught Rom that a regular water spray, and not a water dish is what these snakes require.

Soon many species were breeding and the annual births of pythons, water monitors, crocodiles and finally the king cobra were generally given plenty of press coverage.

The greatest attraction, a fifty metre circumference open enclosure with two to three hundred snakes was a failure, with deaths being unacceptably high. Not enough attention was given to individual feeding idiosyncracies, and the vibrant, diurnal species were constantly disturbing the quieter, less brash crepuscular ones. Chameleons and vine snakes proved to be fragile captives while water snakes and rat snakes were winners: nothing seemed to faze them. Of course, visitors loved this exhibit, with its knots of rat snakes in the branches, bronzeback tree snakes zipping in and out of bushes, and the odd cobra briefly flashing its hood as a chameleon or water snake walked boldly over it.

The centre pit was eventually turned over to a group of water monitor lizards and another more successful exhibit developed with fewer animals and hourly lectures on snakes and snakebite treatment in English, Hindi and Tamil. A south American tarantula was Rom's special pet and lived in a cage adjoining the office for several years, feeding on mice and geckos. One morning Rom was holding it on his palm and a gust of wind from the rotating fan knocked him to the ground, killing him. A college student with him at the time incredulously noted and publicised the fact that Rom's eyes were blurred as he preserved the little fellow in formalin; in any case it was probably one of the best loved tarantulas anywhere.

The Irula hunter, Annamalai, was the main supplier of rats to feed the snakes at the Snake Park and his weekly visits there were an education in themselves: bags with gerbils, field mice, bandicoots. More than once he'd put his rat bags down on the floor of the bus and go to sleep, to find a stampede in progress; the bag had hopped away, and passengers had subsequently hopped off the bus in panic. In fact, through many such rat and snake escape adventures on buses and trains, the gentle, tolerant south Indian mentality has often protected the Irula from being beaten up or severely chastised.

The Irula eat several species of the rodents which abound in the agricultural areas outside of Madras, one instance of their being assisted by the drastic changes in the environment. Rodents are much more canny than snakes and in hunting them the Irula must use his cunning against the rat's deviousness. The gerbil builds long tunnels in its burrow which often extend to several metres. The main feature is an escape route to a distant exit hole. With this species, digging is often of no use. You could dig diligently for hours while the alert rodents skip the country through hidden exit holes you aren't aware of — the entire floor plan of the burrow could cover over fifteen or twenty metres! So the Irula puts down his crowbar and uses an earthen pot which he fills with dry leaves and twigs, lights it and puts the opening over the main burrow hole while he blows from a small opening at the other end. Powerful gusts of smoke surge into the burrow, suffocating the rodents in their holes.

Often of course, snake and rat catching are combined; on seeing a good rat burrow during a snake hunt a group of Irula will separate, and sometimes the rats are cooked out in the open as the group is on its way back from a day's hunt. Rom often participated in the feast, gnawing at a small drumstick and feeling like Gulliver among the Lilliputians.

By the mid 70s the Snake Park was a widely appreciated conservation centre, carrying out vital reptile surveys and engaged in conservation activities which often made it unpopular with local wildlife officials. One of its continuing battles was about Guindy Deer Sanctuary, the last remaining coastal scrub in Madras, which was being steadily depleted by wood poachers and vested interests who disregarded its precious ecological status. As a member of the Tamil Nadu Wildlife Board, Rom kept the fire stoked and suggested several measures to protect the Park permanently. But still, the Cancer Research Institute was given seven acres of prime land within the sanctuary. In 1977 when Mrs Indira Gandhi visited the Snake Park, Harry Miller and Rom talked to her about the depredation of Guindy. Within a few months of her visit it was declared a national park and a wall constructed around it.

Mrs Gandhi was surprised at what she called the 'conservation furore' that the small Snake Park had managed to achieve. But it was exactly this, its compact administration, that was its greatest strength; the absence of laborious procedures made quick, effective results possible. Another favourable factor was that its doors were always open to outsiders with academic or practical zoology interests, and in this way many volunteers who helped out in various ways — from licking stamps to conducting lab research — were able to use the Park as a stepping stone to a full time involvement in projects elsewhere. This arrangement was of course mutually beneficial, giving the organisation a free input of a lot of enthusiasm and energy. D Basu, a Bengali student at the Indian Institute of Technology, Madras, worked on the first crocodile egg collection and rearing programme at the Snake Park and went on to become one of the few qualified croc people in the country. When the combined Government of India and United Nations crocodile project was underway he joined the Uttar Pradesh Forest department and is now in charge of its Gharial Rehabilitation Centre in Lucknow. In the course of his work Basu had the honour of releasing the first gharial hatchlings reared in captivity into the Chambal river. This brought him face to face with the famous Chambal dacoits on more than one occasion, even exchanging words with the bandit queen, Phoolan Devi.

Satish Bhaskar was another IIT drop out who came to Rom with a strong interest in marine biology and a less than strong interest in pursuing his engineering course. He became a field officer at the Snake Park, carrying out the first surveys of sea turtle nesting on beaches on the mainland and off shore island coasts of India and is currently a consultant to WWF-Indonesia; but more of him later. Shekar Dattatri, also studying in Madras, arrived every morning at the Snake Park on the stroke of nine when college classes began, and became Rom's right hand man. He has turned out to be a talented photographer and artist.

But in the general atmosphere of roadside showmanship it was easy for Rom to lose track of the wealth of scientific data that was coming his way, particularly since no one at the Park had the academic background conducive to conduct result oriented science. It was Professor Carl Gans, Rom's mentor-friend, who through his gentle haranguing, put Rom on the track of serious herpetology. Carl is the guru of many herpetologists around the world and one of his passions is an unusual group of snakes found mainly in the hills of southern India. These are the shield tail snakes or uropeltids, little known burrowers which are as significant to evolutionary herpetology as Darwin's Galapagos finches are to ornithology.

Known from two specimens collected in 1912, the cane turtle was rediscovered by Snake Park researchers on a trip to the forests of Kerala in 1982. One of the strangest turtles in India, it lives in the damp environment of the tropical rain forest and dives under leaves to escape predators, the way other turtles dive under water.

In the early 70s Carl was on a visit to south India to look at some of the species he'd never seen before, travelling with a herpetologist from Palayamkottai, Dr MV Rajendran. Rom had arranged to meet them at Kakachi in the Ashambu Hills and providentially just as Carl and Rajendran drove up, he stood up from an over turned log with a handful of wriggling, colourful shieldtails, a sight that must have warmed the cockles of Carl's heart. When I met Carl years later he remained in the category of 'A Scientist' until we spent three tragicomic days together in Kerala and I discovered that he was a mortal after all, and a jolly good one at that.

Not only did Carl encourage the systematic collection of reptiles, he stressed the importance of meticulous record keeping, since so little data was available on reptile ecology and taxonomy from most areas of the tropical world. Not too long ago, for example, Karl Schmidt's tragic death from a boomslang bite had first demonstrated that it was a very dangerous snake. Similarly at the Snake Park Rom discovered that several harmless species, especially in the rear fanged category, could inflict damage. Rear fanged snakes are a large group in India, consisting of twenty tree snakes and seven brackish water snakes. In the evolution of the venom injection systems in snakes these are considered the most primitive. The fangs are merely a pair of enlarged, grooved teeth in the rear of the top jaw. These enlarged teeth are also useful to hold slippery prey like frogs and lizards, and to puncture the inflated bodies of frogs. Although there have been no authentic reports of serious bites from rear fanged snakes in India, some of them, like the Forsten's cat snake, grow to over two metres in length and could be dangerous.

One of the difficulties that Rom faced in those early years was evaluating how best the Snake Park's work could fit in with the general perspective of the conservation movement. It was the only nongovernmental establishment of its kind and it was important to channel its activities into the main flow of national activity as also to avoid, whenever possible, ugly confrontation with wildlife officials. It was difficult to tread the fine dividing line between meaningful conservation activities and deterioration of relations with Forest department officials. Was it really worthwhile creating tornadoes in the press about poaching in Guindy Deer Park or the creation of a new hydel dam project, at the cost of alienating the range officers and wardens he was ultimately so dependent on for snake collecting permits, grants, and the general goodwill necessary to continue his work?

Talks with my father, with whom there was an increasing camaraderie because of the common interest in natural history and conservation, helped put matters in perspective, as did the visits of friends from abroad like Richard and Maisie Fitter of the Fauna and Flora Preservation Society, always ready to listen, advise and encourage. The concensus was generally unanimous, that it was worth sticking one's neck out.

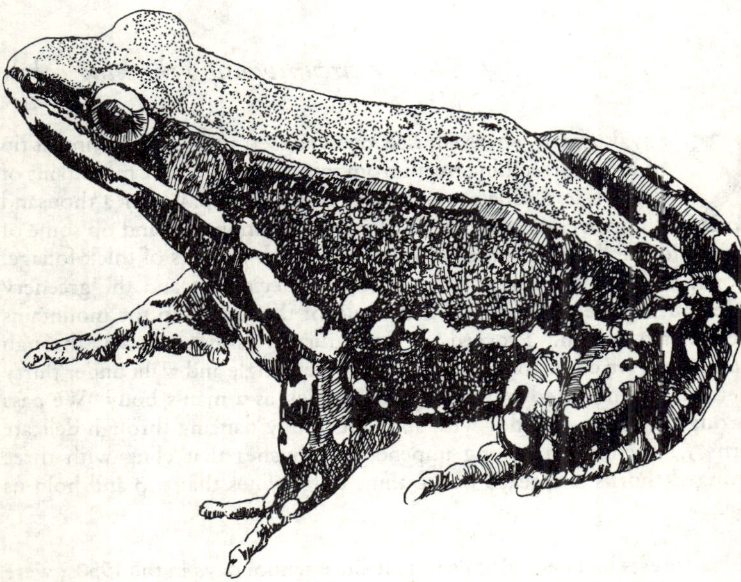

The Malabar frog is one of the colourful denizens of the Western Ghats.

circumventing the king cobra

Kanyakumari, where sunrise meets sunset, is the southernmost tip of India. Stretching north from this point the magic mountains of the Western Ghats wend their way to Bombay over a thousand kilometres of coastline. They catch the monsoon and tip some of it over to the dry east; nine hundred metre high buckets of thick foliage. North of Goa, the forest cover is mostly deciduous and the greenery fades during the dry months. But south of the Goa Gap the mountains are always green. Proceed a little further south, down through Karnataka, we come to large stretches of wet jungle and walk under thirty metre trees embraced by giant vines as thick as a man's body. We pass through an open corridor with sunlight briefly dancing through delicate ferns ... then again among impenetrable bushes that cling with three pronged thorns and reach out to thin, tough vines that trip and hold us back.

These forests had been Rom's retreat since school days in the 1950s; were even, perhaps, the anchor that held him to India. As a child, the ability to become totally absorbed in nature provided a rubber lining that cushioned the impact of an early family crisis which somehow didn't undo him at the seams. He'd just bobbed along beside the typhoon, hunting make believe dinosaurs in the garden, and later real snakes. But to return to the Ghats: these mountains became an adult world refuge, a source of energy and held an escape from traumas otherwise difficult to come to terms with.

The Western Ghats also meant King cobras. These magnificent snakes would excite any herpetologist but Rom's interest was further stimulated by the exploits of the great African snake man, PJP Ionides, in Thailand. This is where the King grew the largest, often reaching five metres in length. With Jon Leakey, son of the famous paleontologist couple LSB and Mary Leakey, Ionides visited southern Thailand in 1966 and they were taken to no less than fourteen King cobra nests in the space of a couple of weeks. The misleading stories about the aggressiveness of these snakes, supported even by naturalists like Jim Corbett — and which Rom takes every opportunity to refute — were torn to bits by Ionides' experiences in Thailand. Females sitting on their nests, which he and his team caught, made no attempt to attack them.

In India practically nothing was known about King cobras, the largest venomous snakes in the world. King cobras feed exclusively on snakes and the most common prey species are rat snakes and water snakes. Slightly less toxic than the common cobra, the venom of the King cobra comes wholesale. The glands can contain 6 or 7 ml, enough to despatch an elephant. There is only one case on record in India of a human death from a King cobra bite. An Englishman named Slater foolishly put his foot on a King cobra's head, was bitten above the knee and died some hours later.

22 March, 1972. Rom and Linda were on their way to the Ghats to spend a few days at Agumbe with their friend David Hayles, who had been living and working at the Snake Park for several months. Agumbe is the Cherapunji of the south, with 7500 mm of annual rainfall and like it, could be completely devastated unless someone heeds the warning and reverses the present trends of heavy timber extraction. Incredibly, Cherapunji with its 10,000 mm rainfall — the highest in India — is now a drought prone area because the forests there have been so drastically plundered for short term gains. A high rainfall encourages a greater diversity of plant species and Agumbe, situated on a little piece of the Ghats that juts out toward Udipi in north western Karnataka, merits greater attention as an important evergreen forest.

One can never be dry in Agumbe; the air is so loaded with moisture that it's like being drizzled on continuously and towels, bed sheets and clothes are always damp. This climate is of course congenial for leeches. I remember my own first visit to Agumbe five years later, with Rom and our friend Ranil Senanayake, the Sri Lankan herpetologist. We sat down to breakfast to find the table had disappeared as in a fairy story... a thick white fog blew in through the door like a genie, and we ate our bread and butter by feeling around like the blind. The other memory of Agumbe is of the cook at the rest house, who blew his nose on the curtain every time he passed by, and also used it as a dish cloth.

When Rom and Linda arrived at the rest house David Hayles was there to meet them on the verandah, which faced the edge of the Ghats: thick jungle in every direction, and the smooth creamy fog surging up from the valley below.

That first day David and Linda stayed at the rest house and Rom took his sleeping bag, a pan, some *rawa* and brown sugar in a knapsack, and walked up a nearby track to find a good camping site. The forest seemed to thicken with every step and soon the trees were choked with orchids and smothered with streamers of lichen which defied the sunlight. Recent timber felling on the periphery had left gashes like pieces of a bombed out city. He stopped near a small stream to make a fire and cook some *rawa* porridge for himself. *Rawa* is a practical camping food; a little goes a long way and it cooks quickly. Although not quite a gourmet's delight, it is a highly nutritious cereal and 'sticks to the ribs',keeping hunger at bay for long periods.

Having eaten, Rom continued on his way. Three kilometres in, then up a westward path towards the edge of the hills. It was the still, silent period of transition between afternoon and evening, when even the tireless crickets and cicadas seem to slow down a bit. Halfway up, a black tail whisked into the thick bushes to the right and Rom, assuming it was a rat snake,instinctively plunged to the ground and grabbed it. But from his prone position he saw a large, hooded snake over three metres long charging at him with open mouth. Taken by surprise, the King cobra growled throatily; Rom's reflexes came to life and he dropped the tail. The big snake immediately stopped its charge and shot back into the bushes.

The chance of a lifetime had slipped away and Rom fell from the pinnacle of excitement with a heavy thud. Breaking off a stick, he followed the snake's tail and feverishly poked a brush pile which seemed the most likely place the snake could be hiding in. The King cobra plummeted out and was off towards another brush pile nearby. Rom grabbed the tail again and this time, as it raised itself for a lunge, he fenced it with a stick, heart beating like a drum. It struck at the stick repeatedly and stood up higher, almost at eye level, its intelligent, disconcerting eyes watching Rom. For the next twenty minutes Rom concentrated on keeping its attention and pulling it back from its efforts at getting away. Soon it began to tire, the lunges were less springy.

This was Rom's cue. With one hand he struggled with his sleeping bag and managed to pull it out, stretch it on the path and prop the mouth open with dry sticks to make a sort of cave. With the other hand he guided the snake toward the opening, offering it an escape from the strange madman blocking its way. It struck and bit the cloth for more endless minutes, then slid into the sleeping bag, and Rom tied the heavy load with shaking hands. This was his biggest triumph so far, but the price could have been heavy. Harry Miller wrote about this adventure in the *Indian Express:* "King cobras possess huge amounts of venom and because they are rare snakes no one in India has embarked on the complex and expensive task of producing an antidote to their venom. If Rom had been bitten, it is unlikely that he could have survived. The catching of so large and fierce a venomous snake, alone and almost literally bare handed, must surely go down in the annals of natural history as an act of almost unbelievable skill and heroism".

The next morning Linda, Rom and David walked ten criss crossing kilometres looking for a camp site. 'A real five star one', said David and found a small stream shaded by giant trees and marked with wild pig, jungle cat and civet tracks. They made the evening fire and brewed strong tea as the day ended with the fantastic sounds of racket tailed drongos, hill mynahs and hornbills. The fire went cold as they slept heavily on flat rocks. In the morning Rom was cooking *rawa* porridge when a cobra went right by Linda's foot as she sat on the bank, watching David dive after watersnakes in the cold stream.

One evening a few days later, Rom was walking down a dry stream bed trying to find his way back to camp. It was getting dark and he'd walked further than planned; a hungry stomach turned him round but the several attempts at shortcuts proved very time consuming. Finally, he found the original path with his own crossed stick landmarks. And as he turned in, there again was the spine tingling sound of a big snake in the leaves ahead of him.

Looking up, he imagined the sound came from a thick cluster of bushes to the side and stepped towards it, stick and large muslin bag ready this time. A split second later there was a movement and a low moaning growl. A four metre King cobra sat straight up ahead of him in the stream bed! The camouflage had worked perfectly and if it hadn't vocalised, Rom might have walked straight into the snake. Standing up over a metre off the ground, it was facing the bushes, showing off its yellow chevron marked hood in a striking defence display.

Once more to the tune of his heart's drumbeat, Rom stepped forward; and the snake immediately rushed into the bushes, barely giving him a chance to grab its tail. As he did so there was a louder growl from the mid body and a sharp hiss. By this time it was securely trapped in the tangle of bushes in the embankment, so they started a ten minute tug-of-war, the snake staring down at its opponent with mouth open. Eventually, Rom managed to pull it free without injury and the snake landed with a thud near his feet; he hastily stepped back. Again, the open mouth charges and another long session of hanging on, dodging out of range and hauling the snake back into the open as it tried to get away.

By now it was almost sundown and the forest lit with the fantastic threads of sunset colours. The technique of propping the bag open didn't work this time, the active snake would not allow Rom to take his eyes off him for a moment. Rom threw the bag at him in desperation, hoping it would slide over its head, but the snake bit it and that was that. Retrieving the bag with his cross stick, which now shook in his fatigued arm, Rom tried once more and this time it landed clear over the snake's head and erect forebody. The King cobra slid neatly inside. Jumping gratefully on the bag Rom clamped it closed after slapping the tail a few times to speed things up. The King cobra and he trudged back to camp in the moonlight, and over vegetable stew and *chappatis* the three of them wondered at the good fortune of finding two of these magnificent snakes in the space of a week.

But cruel disappointment lay ahead. Off the train in Madras, Rom went home to bathe leaving the King cobras in the office and asked an assistant to wet the floor down for coolness. He came back to find the bags themselves had been soaked and the snakes had suffocated to death. Grieved, Rom prepared his once vibrant and plucky rivals for their ignominious end in a formalin jar, becoming even more determined to rear and breed King cobras in captivity. He was sure that if he caught them himself, without pinning the head which is so physically traumatic for the snake, they would do well as captives; and offspring might then replace the large numbers of caught in-the-wild snakes that zoos went through and which the declining wild populations could not sustain. In later years the Snake Park did breed King cobras, for the first time in India.

Rom and Linda were drifting apart; perhaps his single minded interest in natural history left no room and no time to nurture their relationship in the new and strange country. Shortly after the return from Agumbe she went back to America. Rom was back in the jungle with his friend Chris Pruett, a British entomologist who was then making a butterfly and moth collection in south India. Chris wanted to look at the bugs in the Ashambu hills, south of Tirunelveli and Rom went with him to the Singampatti tea estate at Manjolai where they were guests of John Bland and his family. Among the stiff upper lip chota pegs and shining silverware, the two naturalists must have stood out in stark relief, with their mud caked jeans, bloody leech bites and long stringy hair.

The incredible luck held out. On the fourth afternoon they left the jungle at the bottom edge of the estate just before dusk, and stopping for a smoke Rom walked over to the path's edge and looked down a rocky slope just in time to see the now familiar banded form. He whistled to Poolappan, a shikar guide with him that day, and told him to keep an eye on the *Kurra Nagan* while he ran down the path. Descending rapidly, he heard Poolappan yell — 'Watch out, its near your foot!' He looked down in time to move his stick between the snake's head and his bare feet. The three metre female King cobra saw the stick and letting out a hiss, lunged forward pushing its head into a hole in the rocks near by. Rom gently lifted the tail and gripping it firmly, made his way slowly up the steep slope towards the open path. The cross stick strategically placed, protected him. Once on level ground he allowed the snake to let off steam and played the old catch-me-if-you-can game to tire it out. Poolappan meanwhile opened up a specially modified butterfly net frame with visibly shaking hands. He attached the bag to it and held it open on a two metre pole as they manoeuvred the King cobra into it.

A few days later Rom caught its mate, close to the same spot. He knew that sooner or later they would get their heads smashed in if they remained there; King cobras are regularly clubbed or shot in the tea estates which have encroached so extensively on their habitat. Both these specimens became very tame in captivity and were star attractions at the Snake Park. Soon word spread that the Park was interested in keeping King cobras alive, and a few of the managers of tea estates sent specimens which soon died due to the rough handling received at the time of capture. But two were caught with great aplomb and courage by Nikko Rawlley of Mudis tea estate in the Annamalai hills. One of the King

This Andaman watersnake laid its eggs while it was being transported from Port Blair to Madras. It looks very different from the mainland watersnake yet they are supposedly the same species.

cobras had been grabbed by labourers who thought it was a rat snake, a common identity confusion. By the time they discovered their mistake it was a tiger by the tail situation and they were too enmeshed in the snake to let it go. Nikko rescued them by holding the neck and bagging it.

Continuing his quest for the King cobra, Rom visited the Nandankanan Biological Park in Orissa and made friends with the snake keeper, a boy from the famous village of Patia near Bhubaneshwar where a clan of snake catchers specialize in the art of King cobra 'charming'. Together they went to Patia and several of Das' relatives took out their snakes for Rom to photograph. Every year in the winter time these hunters go in groups to the mangrove swamps in Bhitar Kanika to look for King cobras basking in the sun. They catch them with nooses, defang them and cart them across the countryside as far as Delhi and Kashmir — eking out a day to day living by making them 'dance' to their flutes.

Rom had seen the two chunks of King cobra habitat on mainland India, the Western Ghats and the mangrove swamps of Orissa and West Bengal. But the most enticing were the almost legendary jungles of the Andaman Islands in the Bay of Bengal, where these big snakes are commonly sighted and killed, often on their nests. For a while the Islands were out of bounds since Rom was a foreign national and he had to satisfy himself with reading old natural history accounts of these fascinating evergreen forests. In 1975 he became an Indian citizen and a few months later he was in the wet, almost visibly steaming jungles on the island of Middle Andaman. His companion was a Karen (Burmese) boy, Brian Vaughan, who claimed to have seen a big snake lying in a bamboo grove. This was the month of April, reportedly the nesting season of King cobras, the only snakes in the world to build nests. Brian's account could only mean one thing: and they were off together, not daring to waste time in too much preparation.

They stumbled into the thick sheets of April rain, often tripping over spiky bamboo and sliding down slopes. They had to stop frequently to remove the clusters of leeches that burrowed through socks and canvas shoes, soon to become swollen blobs on a toe or ankle; Brian had one hanging from one ear lobe like a bizarre ornament. After an hour he stopped to indicate a dark stand of over-hanging bamboo. 'That's where it was', he said.

Rom was out of breath and panting. Wiping off the sweat and raindrops from his face, his eyes cleared and focussed on a thin but healthy looking King cobra coiled over her carefully tended nest mound. They extracted

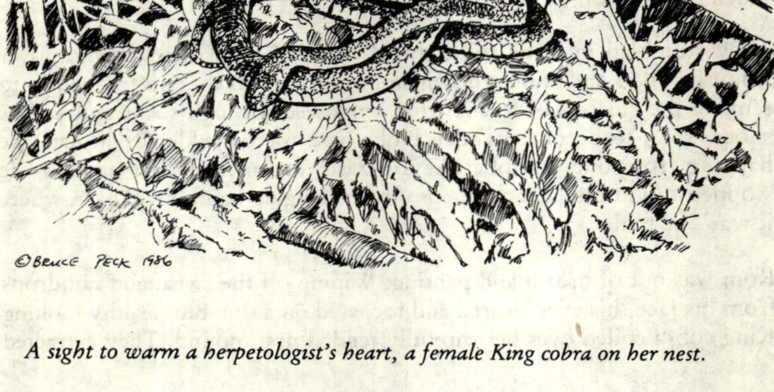

A sight to warm a herpetologist's heart, a female King cobra on her nest.

the camera from layers of protective plastic and took some blurred pictures in the fading light, then sat down to watch her. When finally approached, she slid off into the bamboo without the least sign of aggression or resistance. So much for the deadly attributes of chasing people and unprovoked attacks. The leafy mound was a metre across and as Brian remarked, you couldn't imagine it was the work of an animal with no arms and legs. The surrounding area had been cleared of leaves and humus with sweeps of the snake's body. At the bottom of the nest was a neat cup of leaves like a bird's nest, with nineteen oblong, yellowish eggs. Brian said that the farmer who had discovered the nest planned to come back and destroy them, so they transferred them to a cloth bag lined with leaves and brought them back to Madras.

Rom kept these eggs in a plastic bread box on a bookshelf at home, with holes in the cover for air; unnecessarily large, as it turned out, for on hatching the forty five centimetre long King cobras climbed out and into his collection of Arthur Clarke and Isaac Asimov. It took several hours to collect all the deadly little truants, equipped from birth as they are with fangs, venom and the will to defend themselves by biting. Three of these still survive ten years later and one of the females mated with a male King cobra from the Mangalore Zoo to produce the first captive clutch in the country.

A year later, in 1976 Rom was back to Middle Andaman, this time in mid monsoon and with photographer Rajesh Bedi, to photograph and record the hatching and dispersal of King cobras from a wild nest. They were near the eastern shore of the island at a settlement known as 'Karmatang No.9' and their guide, a Ranchi farmer, had seen the nest several weeks earlier while cutting fence bamboo to protect his rice fields from the ravages of spotted deer and wild pig. He explained, 'My companion poked a stick into this mound of leaves and a big snake appeared and stood straight up with its neck spread out! We ran! Even left all our cut sticks behind! In Bihar there is a snake like this which can burn trees with its breath. We thought it better to get out'.

It was a strenous walk, over logs, wading through streams and trotting gratefully across any flat stretches that came their way, stopping of course to pick off the leeches that constantly appeared, from every direction. And finally a thick bamboo slope where the guide stood aside to let them pass. The rain had flattened the nest and there was no sign of the female. But digging carefully into the mound they found the sixteen eggs. And here again, uncanny luck. They found the eggs were all slitted and several small black noses were emerging into the world. They had hit on the right

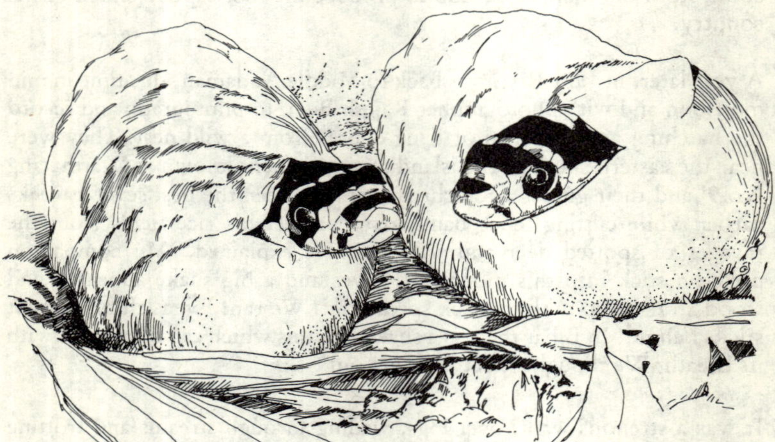

A big breakthrough at the Snake Park was the successful hatching of King cobras. These hatchlings peered out at us from the safety of their egg shells for two days before finally slipping out into the world.

day and the right time to see one of the great natural phenomena of the reptile world unfolding before them. From a crude shelter they watched the hatchings for the next twenty four hours. They were startling, with their miniature hoods and bright black and yellow bands. Without exception, they all headed straight up into the bamboo, as the rain beat down ever so hard on the now empty nest.

coming together

At the World Wildlife Fund office in Bombay, my sister Shama was having problems keeping the show on the road. Although the membership list expanded by leaps and bounds, funds were always short and several worthy projects had to be shelved because of the sleazy question of money. The Bombay Natural History Society generously gave the WWF office space on its premises at Hornbill House. My father had managed to get donations from industrial houses which kept the administrative side rolling and a few studies, such as a survey of the Great Indian Bustard, partly funded. He also collected contributions for the initial propaganda for Project Tiger.

I helped Shama at the Hornbill House office with the routine mechanical work, such as processing memberships, keeping accounts and correspondence. This gave her time for other things — talks on wildlife at schools and colleges, and editing the newsletter. She was also studying for her MA in English literature at St Xaviers College. So WWF became a family affair for a while, with father and ourselves driving to work and back together. My mother, who is a landscape architect and a writer, was Literary Editor for the magazine *Quest,* and her office was just round the corner from WWF. Sometimes we would all meet for lunch. At the time our brother Murad was in Germany, working in Elba Werks in Stuttgart and making cautious advances at a beautiful young nurse he was later to marry.

The easy, informal atmosphere in the office suited me very well. An emotionally crippling nervous breakdown at seventeen had left me in a kind of mental limbo. I had to leave school for a year, and was sent to stay with relatives in Switzerland for a while. But it was a long time before I was mentally and physically well again. During those two invalid years my boy friend, Sajid Peerbhoy, helped immeasurably. Without Sajid's help, love and support, such a complete and early recovery would have been impossible.

At WWF Shama arranged a series of fund raising events, the first of which was a rock concert held at the Taj Hotel in 1970 with the help of several musicians who offered to play gratis. College students turned up in droves, we got many new members and a little money was collected but the overheads were high so the kitty maintained its status quo. Eventually we hit upon the idea of science exhibitions at Hornbill House which could be organised with little expenditure and would generate ticket money as well as public education.

The first one was on common local birds, for which we procured stuffed specimens from the Prince of Wales Museum and, with the help of a group of reliable volunteers, created dioramas which were picturesque if a little scientifically uncertain; kingfishers nested in trees, and a babbler was laying its eggs in a crow's nest. There was a tremendous response from schools and Shama's hourly lecture and slide show was always followed by long question and answer sessions. Some questions were tricky and beyond the scope of our knowledge, so one of us would sprint up to see JC Daniel, the BNHS curator, with a breathless — 'What genus do bee-eaters belong to?' Our activities were largely dependent on the goodwill and assistance of the staff of the BNHS and they never let us down.

The next exhibition, in 1972, was on the common snakes of India and we invited Rom Whitaker from the Madras Snake Park to help with it. He arrived with his Irula friend, Natesan, and over a hundred live snakes. A local carpenter had made plywood pits for the harmless ones and terrariums for the venomous. The response from schools again was overwhelming; for the two booking days specified on the circular one of us was on the phone continuously and, predictably, the appointments went askew on a gargantuan scale. That whole week there was a line of up to several hundred children waiting in the sun.

Over ten thousand children came to the exhibition and learnt about the local species of snakes, how to identify the venomous ones, about the proper treatment of snakebite. We ran out of tickets, information leaflets; Natesan was bitten by a green pit viper and was very sick for a day; all of us became increasingly hoarse, and in the middle of it all Rom broke a tooth and had to go off to a dentist while a sea of hopeful children waited for his talk. The dental gap prevented him from smiling, and a group photograph taken just before he went back to Madras shows him glaring fiercely at the camera, mouth tightly pursed.

And one afternoon during the slide show a small harmless watersnake escaped from its enclosure and crawled through a crowd of intent children. All hell broke loose in the darkened room. School bags and tiffin boxes were thrown aside and burst open with a clatter as the shrieking mob rushed toward the door, which fortunately was ajar. I was at the mike, doing the Hindi translation of Rom's talk, and was almost knocked down as two frightened bodies threw themselves at me, wrapping their legs around my ankles in their bid to leave the ground as fast as possible.

As if the poor students hadn't suffered enough already, Rom burst into an angry tirade after the snake was caught and they filed back into the room. 'Chickens! Cowards!' he yelled into the mike as the repentant refugees looked on in fear, 'We just told you never to panic....'

On the fourth day of the exhibition Rom looked up from a sick python he was cleaning with swabs of cotton wool and asked if I would marry him. I didn't take it seriously but he persisted with all the single mindedness of a naturalist. 'Ten years older, and toothless', I reminded him kindly, but he countered, solemnly, that his new tooth was ready next week and that age was no bar where true love was concerned. I said I was impressed with his philosophy and would think about it.

My parents came back from a month in Europe to find the phone regularly ringing for me and they must have found the sudden interest in snakes a bit unnatural. With their typically quiet concern and consideration, for which Shama and I were to be always grateful, they set about getting to know Rom, and invited him to dinner at our beautiful home in Andheri. Rom brought Natesan along, and asked him to sit beside him at my mother's elegant table. The Chinese lace tablecloth was soon strewn with food as the good man of the jungle flung balls of rice into his mouth and licked his hands to stall the trickling curry. Rom blew his nose with his hand and Natesan dug up a bed of white lilies hunting for rats to take back for their python. But through all this my parents saw very quickly the hard core of Rom's personality and their affection and respect for him was an added incentive to my eventual decision. 'He's a good chap', said my father, a man of few words.

We met occasionally over the next two years and wrote often. My collection of love letters from Rom is mostly treatises on deworming cobras, the difficulties of feeding tokay geckos, the interesting issue of compacted bowels in monitor lizards. At the end there was often a small postscript, "I love you and love you and love you. Could you ask your father to donate the Gir project jeep to the Snake Park?"

Rom was keen on getting married soon but for me it was a difficult decision. I was much better and had regained my equilibrium, but I knew that marrying Rom would mean a life where wildlife and conservation activities dominated and nothing would be allowed to come in the way. Besides, compromises had not been my forte anyway, and marrying Rom would mean a whole new range of adjustments that I didn't feel up to making. My activities and interests were centred in the urban front; at the time we met I was learning the sitar and studying German with hopes of becoming an interpreter; the idea of scraping along on a very basic salary horrified me, and my loving family of four — parents, Shama and brother Murad — would no longer be there to break my falls. To be fair, it was an equally difficult period for Rom; he was taking on a very stormy teenager, used to all the comforts he was unable to provide and one short encounter in between left him rather weak kneed. "Sometimes I wonder", he wrote, "I seem to be taking on a tragicomic character, who may not be very well suited to my own down-to-earth theatre...."

Because of my father's involvement with wildlife conservation work we'd had a lot of Single Minded Naturalists staying with us at our home in Bombay and as a race they hadn't appealed to me overmuch. For one thing, too many came and being neurotically antisocial at that time I was constantly confined to my room waiting for their departure, of which our cook, Paul duly informed me, 'Psst-they've gone. Come out.' How I admired Shama and our brother Murad who boldly sat in the drawing room asking questions and making easy conversation. Of course, there were exceptions with whom I warily struck up friendships; Paul Joslin who was studying the Gir lions, Sir Frank Fraser-Darling, Hari Dang the mountaineer, Sir Peter Scott, Quentin Bloxam of the Jersey Zoo and the wonderful Fitters of the Fauna and Flora Preservation Society among others. And when I was ten or twelve, the frightening news came that the famous naturalist, George Schaller, was coming to stay. I made arrangements with Paul to have dinner in the bedroom for the few days the drawing and dining rooms would be out of bounds. But when friends at school screeched '*The* George Schaller? Is he *really* coming?' I got brave and followed Shama into the sitting room. And he was so nice that I quite forgot myself and even sat next to him at dinner.

About a year after the snake exhibition, Shama and I went to Madras to investigate 'Zai's young man', and arrived at Central Station at the tail end of a heavy two day storm. Large roadside trees had collapsed, whole colonies of huts were flattened and several of the major roads made inaccessible. In the event that Rom could not get to the station we took a taxi but then realized that the Snake Park would be closed and we didn't know his home address. 'Let's try the Snake Park anyway', said Shama, 'there may be a watchman, or somebody else who knows where he lives'. At this the big taxi driver sat up at attention. 'You want *Pambukaran?* You want English Britishman catching snakes?' 'Yes, yes', we said, and after elaborately skirting around the flooded roads we were deposited at a small cottage on Lattice Bridge Road. The *Pambukaran* turned up himself in his little Ford ten minutes later, after a fruitless attempt to get to the station.

Rom told us that a week of great and prolonged excitement had just come to an end at the Snake Park. The biggest marsh crocodile had escaped from his new enclosure, climbed over the three metre chain link fencing and lumbered off into the adjoining Guindy Deer Sanctuary. It had taken up residence in the Duck Pond at the Raj Bhavan, the Tamil Nadu Governor's estate. For five days Rom and his assistants camped on the bank to protect the crocodile from the security guards who were threatening to shoot it. At first Rom tried sneaking around at night with a torch and noosing it, but the croc was too smart for that. Then they tried a trap made of bamboo poles but he shot through it and into the bigger pond, three metres deep in the middle. By this time, news of the *tamasha* had spread and a goodly crowd, complete with peanut vendors, gathered each morning to watch the progress of the exercise. Ideas deteriorated with the situation; a local football team was asked for their uniforms which, tied to poles, were supposed to act as scarecrows to keep the croc in one area. Finally, the fisheries department came to the rescue with a large drag net and the runaway was caught and brought back to the enclosure.

Shama and I spent the mornings with Rom at the Snake Park just down the road from Gandhi Mandapam and adjoining the Forest department's children's park in Guindy Deer Sanctuary. The most interesting enclosure was the central open pit with a moat running along the wall and thickly planted with local vegetation. At first it looked as if there was nothing inside, and people started moving away. But the foliage parted as a large Bengal monitor peered curiously through and the water rippled as a rat snake shot out after a skittering frog. Once your eyes became accustomed to this spotting game, you could spend an hour enjoying the miniature reptile panorama. The bright green vine snakes swayed balefully from side to side if you went too close and inflated their bodies to show the black and white checkered inter-scale pattern, 'Their underwear', Shama explained to tourists. Rom took one out to show us and as he was explaining how harmless and tame they were, it bit him right on cue, first on one hand, then the other. Bronzeback tree snakes gleamed like copper wires as they slipped over branches. In the evening, after the park was closed to public visitation and the jackals of Guindy Deer Sanctuary joined wildly in with the six o'clock siren, we watched Rajamani throw in bags of frogs for the snakes. Each species caught its prey in its own way: fast or slow, sure or blundering.

Behind the palm leaf structure of the office and laboratory were a row of cages for the Big Four common dangerous snakes of India, the cobra, krait, Russells viper and saw-scaled viper and the snakes from other countries which periodically came in gift parcels from Rom's friends. There were diamond-back rattlesnakes from Heyward in South Carolina, African puff adders from Jan Nedved in Czechoslovakia, pit vipers from Ranil Senanayaka in Sri Lanka, mamushis and habus from Yoshio Sawai in Japan, and others. There was a large and very attractive tank for sea snakes in which the narrow headed and banded sea snakes, two of the common species of the east coast, swam ceaselessly around, as if searching for an eternally missing object. 'Let them go', we said, to Rom's horror.

What a beehive of activity the place was! Public education, research and conservation were always at the forefront and no detail related to these objectives, however small, was ignored. Every letter and query about snakes was answered — and there were hundreds every month including barely comprehensible postcards, obviously written by village 'scribes'. "I am afraiding too much of my wife who has killed a snake in the today. Is it true the snake will come for avenging purposes?" There were letters in practically every language of India, Bengali, Malayalam, Marathi, Kannada, Oriya, Telegu, Gujarati... but we found that every one of these was meticulously translated and answered.

One evening, at tea time, Shama and I were offered a dainty bowl of little brown fried snacks which were delicious until we discovered they were termites. They'd been hunted by Rajamani, one of the Irula snake catchers for whom the premonsoon weather in Madras was termite time. Since there had been a lull in the rains for several days Rajamani planned to try his luck again and we went along as well.

Eesel are the winged adult termites which leave their mounds and swarm on their nuptial flight during the rains. This spontaneous fountain of protein from the ground is a universal treat for a wide range of animals which gorge themselves silly on these insects: frogs, squirrels, mongooses, jackals, birds, scorpions. And in south India, the Irula join them, squatting beside the mound and often popping live termites into their mouths. Rajamani once came upon a swarm in the forest and sat down to eat. Soon a jackal appeared and the two of them amicably shared the feast from opposite sides of the mound. Termites are eaten in many parts of the world but elsewhere, people have to wait for them to swarm. The Irula, on the other hand, have a 'trick' with which they call the cards and make termites emerge early, thus ensuring that they are there to trap them.

It is a muggy night. Now and then a breeze blows, the clouds shift apart, a star flashes briefly. Rom, Shama and I set off with Rajamani, who has found a 'ripe' mound, one in which the termites are ready to swarm. 'These people are ready to come out', he says, using the typically Irula anthropomorphic idiom for animals. The mound we are about to terrorize turns out to be a *katta puthu,* the most common *puthu* or termite nest in the Madras region and also the largest. Some *katta puthus* are as tall as a man and three metres in circumference. This is one of the four varieties of termite mounds that the Irula classify. The others are *kavaram, patti* and *kerian*.

The last, which is inhabited by a species of large, blackish termite and which lacks the exit holes typical of the others, is ecologically the most interesting. It is in the *kerian puthu* that the monitor lizard of south India, the Bengal monitor, often lays its eggs, tunneling into the side of the mound and leaving the eggs to the care of these aggressive termites with their optimum incubation chamber. On hatching, the baby lizards make their exit hole in the top of the mound.

The *katta puthu* Rajamani takes us to is just under two metres high with terraced towers and balconies, like a miniature Spanish castle. With the mosquitoes out in full force we sit down to wait as Rajamani performs his customary prehunt pooja with a piece of camphor. He is very superstitious and of late he has been seeing a small little midget ghost with blue hair near his home in Chitlapakkam. 'He follows me every night, when I go out to relieve myself', he says despairingly.

But at the moment ghosts are far from his thoughts as his wife, Lakshmi ties an old sari around the *puthu* to protect it from the periphery of the mound. Then he wedges a large cooking oil tin into the hole. Over the opening he makes a bridge with two crossed twigs, places an oil lamp on this, lights it. Rajamani then sits down to light a *beedie* and a yawn escapes me. 'What are you waiting for?' I ask, in broken Tamil, unable to curb my urban impatience. 'For me — of course. You Bombay people, you want everything to go like this', he says snapping his fingers.

Finally, the *beedie* is thrown down. A largish brown seed is roasted over the lamp fire and ground into powder on a stone. Rajamani walks around the castle of mud blowing the seed dust into the hundreds of tiny holes which dot its surface. 'This is the magic powder', he explains. 'It tricks the termites into thinking its raining, that its time to come out'.

Half an hour later my legs have gone to sleep but I dare not fidget and risk further aspersions on my Bombay brand of impatience. Rajamani circles the mound again, sprinkling the seed powder and making a whirring sound by vibrating his lips, which is the frenzied noise of swarming termites. At intervals he calls, 'Come out, come out, its raining, come quickly'. He peers into the little exit holes as he walks about. 'Come here. Something is happening there ... these people have started moving.'

We apply our faces to the mud walls and squint into the tiny peep holes. There is definitely a hasty brown activity going on in there. Lakshmi takes a look. 'These are the workers', she says. 'It is their duty to stop the eesel from going outside until they are sure the time is right'.

Another wait, then the first winged termite — our prey — flies across our vision, straight towards the light, and falls into the can. '*Seri* — they are coming. The *sel,* worker ants, have given them permission'. A few more emerge singly and taxi towards the light, like small aircraft before take off. Then the deluge. They start pouring out of the holes, oozing forth in a continuous stream. They create a living road towards the light and in less than five minutes the tin is full and Lakshmi empties it into a gunny sack. Rajamani squats down beside it and starts eating live termites, periodically spitting out the wings which collect in a corner of his mouth. Rom and I hesitantly follow suit, but get our tongues bitten and give up. Now the air is thick with termites, the can a fluffy mass of wings again.

Rajamani points to a large, warty Indian toad a few feet away. He is busy mouthing termites; soon he is far too full to move and just sits there, looking ill. A black scorpion and several geckos Rajamani calls *puthu balli,* join the party, and Rajamani generously moves aside to let them eat their fill, while Shama and I maintain a wary distance. When we leave an hour later the gunny sack is almost full. Next morning Lakshmi will separate the wings, fry the termites, sell some and keep the rest for her family.

At the Snake Park Rom's day was interrupted several times by visitors who had special questions to ask and an enthusiasm that was too much for the watchman who was under instructions to keep people away from the office. The cross section included diplomats, politicians, heads of state, doctors, journalists (always more interested in his personal life than in his work: 'do you like Indian girls') and a variety of witch doctors and travelling mendicants who came to disprove the medical monopoly of antivenom serum. While Shama and I were there a swami arrived and offered to sing his snakebite mantra in the middle of a busy morning. Closing his eyes he launched into a crescendo which brought people running in concern. He was not pleased when, half an hour later, we suggested he'd better shorten his mantra to ensure his patient's survival.

We also found that the Snake Park's work, its routine lectures, publications, and general commotion about reptile protection had created a climate of reptile consciousness in India and popularized snakes and their value in the environment. In Madras it was becoming usual for people to telephone the Park for a catcher to come and collect a cobra or rat snake from a house or garden instead of killing it. This was soon to become a regular organised activity of the Park for a fee of fifteen rupees. Families came again and again to learn to identify the different species and many young school and college students spent holidays there, becoming proficient in handling snakes. The publication a few years later of Rom's field guide to common Indian snakes, helped the tide along and its sales success indicated the growing interest in snakes and their natural history and ecology. A reader from Nagpur made a flattering comparison between it and Dr. Salim Ali's bird book. "Much smaller and less comprehensive as it is, it is having the same sort of effect on people already interested in wildlife but for whom snakes have always been taboo. People like me who had to depend largely on scanty, out dated information, now have something concrete to fall back on and what pleasure it gives the amateur to be able to identify, without doubt, the species around him".

Snake stones are symbols of fertility and are believed to work miracles in south India.

During our recce at the Snake Park Shama and I, very much city kids who knew little about folklore and beliefs, would trail after visitors taking in the wealth of snake myths circulating at the enclosure walls as species after species was spotted and its own peculiar attributes related. As in many other countries, people in India both venerate and fear snakes. At the Perayur temple near Pudukottái, we later saw hundreds of *pambu kallus* or snake stones which were brought by women as offerings, in order to have male children. On the other hand, snakes were mercilessly killed for profit. A ten minute drive away, thousands upon thousands of snake skins changed hands every Friday, generating a thriving skin trade.

Snakes play an important role in Hindu mythology and dazzling legends feature many courageous, trecherous and powerful *bhu-jag*, which in Sanskrit means born of the earth. In the glorious underworld, snakes wear gems in their five, seven or nine hoods. These snake rulers are called *nagas*, which is still the Hindi word for cobra. The king of the *nagas* is Ananta, the Everlasting or Immortal one. He is, of course, eternal, and is often used by Vishnu, the Preserver of the Hindu Trinity, to lie on. When Vishnu was incarnated as the child Krishna, Ananta went along with him and protected him from à storm, with his several hoods.

My sister Shama, who has studied Hindu mythology, writes of Ananta: "He remains with Vishnu even during the periodic destruction of the world. As soon as the world is washed away, the serpent acts as a raft for Vishnu to float on the primeval waters till creation is effected again. While creation is in existence, it is his hoods which support the world and the heavens and he himself is coiled on the back of a gigantic tortoise floating on cosmic water. This is why several temples, in the centre of the floor, have a small unexpected carving of a tortoise, and many an unwary tourist has come to grief on this while admiring the temple ceiling".

A herpetologist travelling around India would be very pleased to see how many reptiles he meets up with in the Hindu religion. The gecko is revered in a rock carving in Kanchipuram in Tamil Nadu. At Konarak in Orissa, a stone crocodile emerges from the side of the Sun Temple with a fish in its jaws. Ganga rides a crocodile or gharial and Jumna, a soft shelled turtle in the temples of Agra and Varanasi. But the cobra is the dominant reptile figure in temple carvings all over India and they range from the many hooded *Sheshnag* to the represenation of rivers as *nagas*.

Against this background there is an exaggerated myth for practically every snake. The red sand boa, which has an absurdly blunt tail, is called the two-headed snake and people swear that it travels first in one direction for six months, then in the other. The slate grey common sand boa, because of its blotched, spotty pattern is said to cause leprosy and the vine snake is called *kunn-kuthi pambu*, eye-pecking snake. The bronzeback tree snake is credited with one of the most colourful myths; it will bite someone, then climb a high tree to wait for the victim's funeral pyre! But the classic Indian snake myth, exploited regularly by the film industry, is the revenge story. Kill a cobra and its mate will seek vengence. And the rustic imagination carries it further: you must burn the dead snake as the last image it sees, it's killer, will remain as a 'foto' in the dead snake's eyes, so that the snake knows who to follow!

Lizards are equally the target of naive beliefs, in fact the house gecko has an awesome reputation and is supposedly responsible for a lot of sickness and even death. "Lizard falls in food: 30 wedding guests in hospital" is a typical headline in newspapers and the innocent reptile is a convenient scapegoat for food adulteration. With surprising ignorance, journalists report, again and again, the same story; the *Indian Express* of 18 October '85: "About 200 children were admitted to hospital following complaints of vomiting and giddiness after taking noon meal (sic). One child was stated to be in a serious condition. A lizard was reportedly found in the meal".

Our preliminary survey of Rom accomplished, Shama and I were on our way back to Bombay and just as the train started moving forward Rom pressed a procupine quill necklace into my hand. 'Next June, then?' I looked hesitantly at Shama. 'Your sister is most welcome to come and live with us,' said Rom gallantly, and we were off.

In Bombay I began to dither again and a college friend urged me to stop it; 'you love the guy man, go for it.' So I burned my bridges and sailed on. We were married in 1974 and after an initial period of difficulties, we became the happiest couple in the whole world. Our coming together was the door to the real me, and if the corridors were a bit musty, the sunlight at the other end was all the brighter.

By this time my parents had sold our large, fairy tale house and garden in Bombay and moved to quieter and climatically more pleasant Bangalore, comfortingly close to Madras. My brother Murad was back from Germany and also lived there. The family was slowly seeping southward, except for Shama who was teaching at a college in Bombay and had her own apartment on Pali Hill, the cosy haven of Hindi film stars. In fact,

Shortly after signing away my life and liberty in June, 1974.

she had one or two of those in her building and lay awake many a night to the sounds of breaking glass and theatrical fights.

Our parents were looking for farm land outside of Bangalore, on which Mother would build a dream house and garden and Father raise a dream horse or two. This happily came to pass, but for the first two years they lived in a rented house at Palace Orchards, adjoining the Raman Institute.

This was where Rom and I got married. Our wedding was an exercise fraught with uncertainty. As, for example, whether Rom would turn up at all. He had given us a date — June 9th — and gone off to Corbett National Park for six weeks. But the Registrar of Marriages was only available on June 7th, so Father booked him but was unable to contact Rom. We had no idea which part of Corbett he would be camping in. Finally, he sent a telegram to every corner of Corbett, saying "You getting married 7 June Bangalore stop You must repeat must get back in time".

Rom got back to Madras in good time to drive Doris, Neel and Nina to Bangalore for the big day. But this was the time of the major petrol crunch and on that day gas stations were hoarding their petrol in anticipation of a favourable price hike. The marriage party was delayed by over ten hours and arrived in Bangalore in the middle of the night, well after we had given up hope.

The ceremony itself was short and simple. We signed quickly, without the usual accompanying speech about 'in sickness and in health' because the Registrar had to rush to another wedding. The little wedding breakfast had been beautifully arranged by my mother, with only a handful of friends and relatives invited. Among these was our uncle Salim, the birdman, and he kept us all roaring steadily with his witty conversation. In the evening there was another party on a much bigger scale and I tried my usual party trick of slinking behind Shama, hoping nobody would see or want to talk to me. Halfway through, the doorbell rang and I raced down the steps (everyone was on the terrace) gratefully. It was a friend of a friend of my parent's, who had come to see them unaware of the occasion. Hearing the jolly sounds from the terrace, he enquired what was going on. 'A wedding', I said — 'Whose?' he asked. 'Mine'.

Two days later, Rom borrowed some money from his new father-in-law and we drove to Nilambur Valley in the foothills of the Nilgiri for a three or four day camp. It was a very beautiful day; an early morning shower had cleansed the foliage with gleaming wetness which made the forest dance and twinkle. The tree trunks and branches of the massive rain forest trees were hung with mossy creepers, epiphytes and lichen. The persistent, pulsing sounds of the cicadas and crickets were like an orchestra of tiny harps and violins — 'Here at last is the church organ', said Rom. We'd driven into a narrow mud road which ended half a mile in where a huge *Bombax* had fallen across it. As we collected our gear the drizzle changed to a downpour, as if on a sudden impulse. Drops of rain trickled down my back. 'Can't we wait until it stops?' 'It won't, it rains here all the time during the monsoon'. Sadly, I eased myself out of the dripping vehicle and plodded down the track hung with knapsack, sleeping bag and water canisters.

We left our gear under a rock overhang and started upstream. Rom was especially keen on finding hump-nosed and Malabar pit vipers for the Snake Park and crawled on hands and knees under the overhanging clumps of ferns and bracken. Pit vipers are often coiled in the cool tangle of the undergrowth, waiting for a frog or lizard to come along. This slow creeping along gave me an entirely new perspective of the jungle. My father is an ornithologist and when out with him we were always looking up into the branches and I now found we'd missed one stratum of the forest altogether: the intricately meshed microhabitats and small details of jungle fabric on the forest floor.

Once we tuned in to our surroundings we were amazed at just how plentiful these statuesque little snakes are in this small tract of evergreen forest. Malabar pit vipers are partial to the edges of the steep hill streams and although they often lie in the open, they are easy to miss. The smaller ones like to hang on low plants and bushes where they blend in very well. The larger ones, forty five centimetres in length, have lichen patterned backs and look more like roots than snakes when you first spot them. A year earlier, Natesan and Rom had found thirty eight of these pit vipers in one morning on a stream near Nilambur, the location of which Rom wants to keep secret. 'It would easily be hunted out if someone suddenly got interested in pit vipers; let's hope it survives the forest clearance and agricultural development in the hills'.

The hump-nosed pit viper is a species also common in parts of Sri Lanka. We found them on the forest floor, often on or near a rock or at the base of a big tree, just sitting there, perhaps patiently waiting for prey. Later, we found one which had swallowed a frog and another which had a gecko inside it, probably a diurnal tree gecko. Ten years later Rom drove a group of 'herp' people to Nilambur after the IUCN Snake Group meeting in Madras and in a few hours they saw a dozen pit vipers; it was

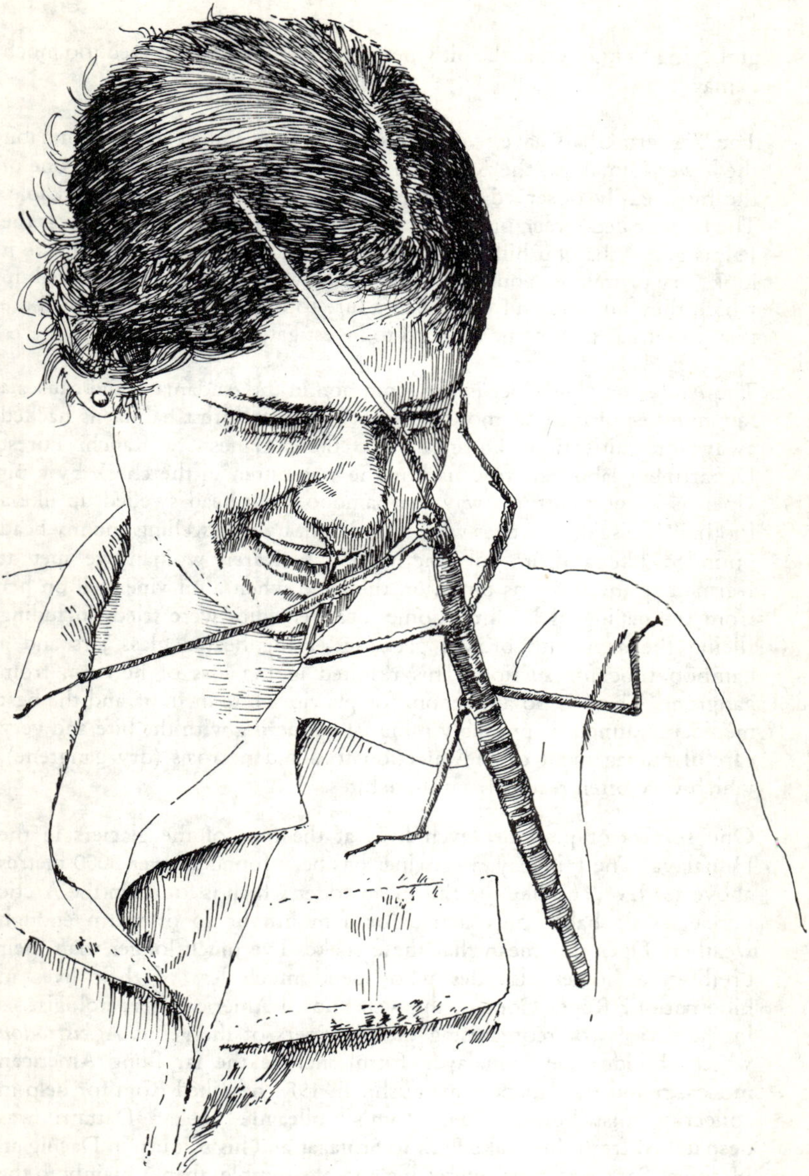

A giant stick insect showers affection on me in Kalakkad during a strenuous honey-moon trek.

gratifying to know that the pit viper population hadn't suffered too much damage.

The Western Ghats have five species of pit vipers and eleven more inhabit the lower Himalaya, the Andaman and Nicobar Islands. They are one of the most easily observed forest snakes and some are quite remarkable. The large scaled, green pit viper is common in some hilly areas such as the Palnis and Ashambu hills. Its large, platelike overlapping scales make it look very primitive. Young pit vipers usually have a light coloured tail tip which they hold up and wriggle as a lure to frogs and lizards, which are then caught as they come forward to investigate.

The Anderson's pit viper is very common in the Andamans and causes a fair number of bites as more and more of their forest habitat is hacked away for cultivation. During a trip there Ganesh, a Ranchi Forest Department labourer, told us how he was bitten in the cheek by a pit viper as he was cutting away the bamboo. 'My head swelled up like a football', he said, 'my eyes were sealed tight by the swelling and my head pounded like a drum for one week'. A Karen woman we met at Karmatang in 1975 was bitten on the hand when a pit viper fell on her from the ceiling of her hut. Some local remedies were tried, including slicing the arm with broken glass and using heated glass jars and a bamboo tube for suction. This resulted in the loss of her arm from gangrene. There is no antivenom for pit viper bite in India and the best medical treatment is probably minimal tampering with the bite and very careful management of the infection to avoid necrosis (dry gangrene), which very often results from these bites.

One species of pit viper even lives at the foot of the glaciers in the Himalaya. The Himalayan pit viper has been found at over 5000 metres above sea level and like the European adder which is found in the Arctic Circle, is probably only active for a month or so of warm enough weather. Does this mean that these snakes live much longer than their brethren at lower altitudes who spend much less of their lives in hibernation? Roger Conant, the well known American herpetologist, is in the process of reorganising the pit vipers of the genus *Agkistrodon* which, besides the Himalayan form, include the far flung American moccasin and the Japanese mamushi. In 1984 he asked Rom for help in collecting distribution data. Rom's colleague Shekar Dattatri was despatched from the Snake Park to Srinagar and his sojourn in Dachigam National Park was most interesting and pleasurable, thanks mainly to the Chief Wildlife Warden, Mir Inayatullah. Shekar found several of the large heavy set leventine vipers and a few Himalayan pit vipers. A month later

Dr Conant and his wife visited Madras and were able to see and photograph them for the first time.

But back to our honeymoon. Three or four hours later that same morning we had crossed the stream several times and my smart new walking shoes, part of the wedding trousseau, were causing considerable anguish. Rom motioned me down to a cave into which he jabbed a stick, and a throaty growl started immediately, like the purr of a giant cat. 'King cobra!' I shouted, caught between fright and excitement. Obviously pleased with this ignorant response, Rom reached down and pulled up a large and very angry rat snake. It continued to growl and strike wildly but with mouth closed and I pulled out a snake bag and held it open. But just then he saw a vine snake on a bush behind me and thrusting the snake into my arms, dived after it. My charge bit me twice, quick smart, and was poised for a third strike. I was about to throw it down when Rom returned with the vine snake and managed to bag them both. We turned back — it was late afternoon and I was exhausted and by now, quite frantic about the ever increasing procession of leeches feasting on my blood. 'Enjoying your honeymoon, sweetheart?' asked Rom as I limped down to the stream on blistered feet to wash off the blood.

We found a gently sloping rock face to sleep on, the slope ensuring that we had to wake up every hour to haul ourselves up like ungainly caterpillars lest we ended up in the stream. At my insistence Rom made a fire to keep elephants away; we'd seen too many large, fresh droppings that day for my comfort. Nevertheless, a big bull came within ten metres of our rock, leaving his large, pancake footprints in the slushy mud of the stream bank. My diary entry for June 10, '74 reads: "It was not a romantic night". And the conversation, mostly about pit vipers, was not romantic either; but it was the beginning of a strong interest in reptiles which was to be one of the cornerstones of our marriage.

Soon after we spent a wonderful few days with Nikko and Meena Rawlley, in the Annamalais, whose thoughtful hospitality and ready participation in our walks around the area we have always remembered with gratitude. Staying with people while engaged in any sort of field work is difficult at the best of times and we have regretted many a stay with finicky hosts who objected to small details, like collections of snakes in the bedroom and the consistent failure to arrive at meals on time. But the Rawlleys were different, they even turned a blind eye to the very destructive antics of my two mongooses who travelled with us. In fact, the male mongoose created a furore the evening after our arrival. We came back from a nearby forest tract to find the female contentedly chewing Meena's best linen, but no sign of him. He was gone; but the doors had been closed and as an afterthought I peered into the toilet bowl — and let out a shameful screech which brought the household on the run. Rom picked him out, turned him upside down and drained him; in five minutes he was conscious and lapping a saucer of Nikko's brandy.

Back at the Snake Park, Rom threw himself into the usual administrative tangles which had developed during his absence and I began editing and putting together reports on the status and ecology of the mugger or marsh crocodile, for which he had gathered information over the last few years. This sort of final putting together of raw material became my special responsibility at the Park and fulfilled both a need there, as well as my own interest in writing and editing. Two years later I started a small newsletter for herpetologists called *Hamadryad* which very quickly took off with support (and funds) from interested people all over the world. The other avenue, cultivated with a fair amount of success, was popular natural history writing for children and adults and it is in this field that my interests are put to their most satisfying use.

A week after we got to Madras, Rom announced that it was time for the second phase of our honeymoon and we went to one of his favourite jungles in the south, the Kalakkad Reserve in the Ashambu Hills, where he had caught two King cobras and helped his friend Chris Pruett with his butterfly and moth collections. We were fortunate in travelling up the ghat road with Tom Struhsaker of the New York Zoological Society. He was on his way to visit Steve Green who was studying lion-tailed macaques, one of the rarest primates in the world. Steve was staying at one of the Manjolai tea estate guest houses at Kakachi and we spent an evening with him before leaving for Sengeltheri, our destination. He had finally acclimatized the macaques to his presence, and was now able to approach those which had earlier been so rigorously hunted that they took fright and fled at the distant approach of a human. A day before our arrival Steve had watched a young male lion-tail catch a forest agamid lizard and chomp it like a breadstick.

At 4.30 the next morning we started off on the Sengeltheri track, a walk of about seventeen kilometres. Today there is a motorable road from the plains to Sengeltheri and the forest is badly degraded compared to what we walked through thirteen years ago. The thick undergrowth and hardwood buttresses were dotted with the remains of abandoned tea and cardamom estates and the animals were making a comeback. Once, a sambar stag dashed through the trees a few metres ahead of us, rearing back momentarily as he saw us, catching his balance like a trapeze artist and flinging himself forward. The leeches seemed to like it here too; at first we kept stopping to pull them off, then gave up. They had no problems penetrating our socks and wriggling in through the shoelace holes. Then they'd begin their march upward, getting fatter and fatter as the blood feast progressed. After an hour the cold, wet feeling behind the knees had to be investigated and the bloated leech pulled off. Over the years we tried all the leech repellents, from soap to kerosene and even invented a concoction of snuff and petroleum jelly that seemed to have possibilities. But nothing worked and our legs have numerous permanent scars to remind us of the festering sores that develop from hosting repeated leech feasts.

We took our time getting to Sengeltheri, investigating streams and collecting two pit-vipers too well fed to put up resistance at their capture. The stick insects of these hills often span over a foot in length and one calmly climbed on to me while we rested under a tree. At first I thought it was a twig but when flicked it began to walk determinedly forward. With him still trekking down my head and shoulders, we scanned the adjoining slopes and cliffs for Nilgiri tahr, the unique wild goat of the southern highlands, but with no luck. Eager to catch at least a small glimpse of the animals we stayed on, making a fire for tea. 'Jungle tea', shouted Rom as he gave me a warped tin mug with steaming liquid. He stirred in a leaf-full of sugar with a twig and we sat back to watch the slopes and the incredible avian panorama in front of us. Scarlet minivets flitted about in their bright red coats, velvet fronted nuthatches crept up nearby tree trunks, sunbirds flew past with flashes of brilliant colour. A splash of yellow-gold as a golden backed woodpecker landed vertically in front of us;the strong, clear whistle of the whistling schoolboy, and the shama composing a song in the dense branches overhead.

With this sort of easy loafing progress it was dusk before we'd gone too far and Rom found another pit viper which we watched stalking and catching a frog, moving in slow motion along a wet, ferny bank so as not to frighten it away. By the time we made it back to the original track it was dark and we found we'd missed the turning west towards Sengeltheri. Rom went back to try and locate it while I sat on my knapsack for half an hour counting the minutes and wondering anxiously whether leopards were still prevalent in these hills. He came back with the good news that our turning was a short distance away so we could cook dinner by the stream, and be in Sengeltheri after half an hour's walk by torch light.

What a luxury it was paddling in the cold stream, waiting for the rice and dal to cook. 'Let's live it up, eh' — and Rom extravagantly threw a potato into the mixture. Lunch had been a one square inch cube of Japanese army survival rations, so the mush tasted like a royal feast, and at nine, we washed our plates, dried them on our jeans, put on sodden keds and hauled up our knapsacks.

Suddenly a few choice words split the silence ending with, 'Bloody torch — where's the bloody torch — I'm sure I bloody packed it'. Rom was scrabbling through the contents of his knapsack which, the embers of our fire showed, did not include the spotlight we'd been depending on. That was bad enough; visions of elephants and panthers crowded my brain. But to add fuel to the fire, Rom burst into a helpless roar of laughter. My frightened expression, he said, was so funny.

We made it finally, to the decrepit old forest rest house with a wood torch, like a small Olympian team:and in my anxiety I stuck to Rom like a leech, tripping him up as my feet scurried in time to his steps. And at the end of that we found the door of the rest house locked; a stained cyclostyled sheet pasted on the door proclaimed in government language the lengthy procedure for booking a room and the list of tariffs. Rom must have sensed my fatigue and anxiety working up to an explosion and took out his Swiss army knife. 'Calm down, we're staying here', and he proceeded to pick the lock with suspicious expertise. As the rusty hinges fell away he ceremoniously bowed me into a room reeking of rat and bat droppings. And that was the tail end of our honeymoon.

Our home is on one of the main turtle nesting beaches on the Coromandel coast. Every year several ridleys make their way up the beach and lay their eggs near our front gate.

sea turtles

Midnight, first week December 1975. The early evening shower had left a damp chill which, combined with the heavy sea spray, made us wish we'd brought along our sweaters. The phosphorous laden sand threw up gleaming, turquoise sprays as our feet kicked it; and the waves were masses of liquid silver. Even the watery half moon seemed to glow unnaturally in this fairy world.

A few metres ahead of us Valliappan stopped, bent down attentively, then strode ahead again leaving a blazing wake of phosphorous. This was the first 'turtle walk' of that winter nesting season of sea turtles, when hundreds — formerly thousands — of olive Ridley sea turtles come ashore to lay their eggs on the Madras coast. With the help of interested people like Valli, Rom had organized a conservation project for this beleaguered turtle which was rapidly declining in numbers because of the heavy, uncontrolled collection of its eggs for the market. The leathery ping pong ball eggs sold for three or four paise each. And the efficient collectors often gathered them as they dropped into the fifty centimetre deep nest hole the female had laboriously dug. Rom and Valli's survey during the previous (1973-74) nesting season told a rather grim story, that over ninety percent of the eggs were taken by dogs, humans and jackals.

Sea turtles are being conserved in Tamil Nadu by the forest department. Eggs collected on the beach at night are incubated in fenced enclosures and the hatchlings are released into the ocean soon after they emerge from the egg.

Given the natural predation levels in the sea, some scientists claim that only one in a thousand hatchlings reach adulthood and it seemed that every effort was needed to discourage the illegal trade in eggs, if the species was to continue nesting on our coast. 'It looks bad for Mrs Ridley', said Valli as he pored over their increasingly depressing data.

To arrest this depredation of eggs and to create a public and official awareness about the plight of this sea turtle on the beaches, we set up a small hatchery at a friend's beach side garden where eggs were brought and buried in simulated nests. Jean and Janine Delouche were delighted when they hatched sixty days later, and the hatchlings were released into the ocean. For four years, volunteers from the Snake Park collected an increasing number of eggs, eventually reaching fifteen thousand eggs of which nine thousand hatched and were released. Later, the programme was adopted by the World Wildlife Fund branch in Tamil Nadu, the state Forest Department and the Central Marine Fisheries Research Institute, and carried out on a much larger scale.

This particular night we hadn't planned to go turtle walking but Valli was sure that nesting would begin earlier than it had the year before. 'I feel it in my bones, man', he said tapping his elbow confidently. So we'd driven south of the city and left the jeep at Thiruvanmiyur around nine o' clock, walking briskly out to cover the longest distance possible before the optimum nesting period between midnight and two in the morning. After a while the soft sand becomes uncomfortable as it gives way and strains the foot muscles, so we walk along the water's edge where the sea soaks in to make a hard pavement. Now, just after midnight, we see an egg collector coming along from the opposite direction with his thin wooden pole with which he jabs the nest area to locate the eggs. It is cruelly easy to find nests; the prominent, churned-up track of the female as she comes ashore and returns to the ocean, makes a V shaped mark and is as good as a signboard. She lumbers about twenty metres up the beach, digs a nest hole, lays her eggs and goes back into the water. The nest is at the apex of the V.

The egg collector had been luckier than us; he'd already collected four nests, about five hundred eggs, and now he couldn't carry any more so was on his way home. This, really, is the only thing the Ridley has to be grateful for:that a man can carry only so much and no more.

We found a stranded narrow headed sea snake on the beach and Rom caught it by the tail and threw it back into the sea. Its survival was doubtful, though — it had been out of water too long and was almost too weak to move. Its breathing apparatus was not designed for extended periods out of the ocean's buoyancy. The year before, on another turtle walk we'd found two banded sea snakes and taken them home to add to the Park's collection. We had no bag or container and the deadly venomous snakes had slithered around loose on the jeep floor while I hugged my knees, eyes glued to the banded forms. During the night at home they'd escaped from their buckets — 'They can't possibly climb out, don't worry', Rom had assured me — and were lying on the pile of washing near the sink in the morning.

On this walk Valli came to an abrupt halt ahead of us and jerked his thumb triumphantly. Fifteen metres ahead was a dark boulder walking ponderously out of the water. At this initial stage of the nesting sequence sea turtles are often very timid, turning back if disturbed by a strange object or sound; but once actual nest excavation begins even an earthquake might not interrupt the determined female. We stood like statues watching her progress up towards the dry sand. 'Let's go', said Valli when she stopped and began to excavate a 'body pit' and we ran and flopped down by her side. I got a faceful of sharp dry sand as she tossed it back with her hind flippers. Once she had shifted the upper layer, the earnest systematic digging of the nest hole began and about thirty minutes after she had left the water, the half metre deep nest hole was ready. This strenuous terrestrial activity made great demands on the stamina of the turtle and she breathed in deep gulps punctuated by short sharp whistles. The water from the lacrymal glands which washed the eyeballs streamed down to give her a tearful look.

A five minute rest period, then the eggs started appearing. Widening the rim of her nest we had a clear view of the cloaca suspended over the nest hole and of the eggs dropping in. Round, white, smooth and bouncy. They came within seconds of each other, sometimes two or three at once. As the hundredth fell in, three jackals stealthily appeared from the casuarina stand bordering the beach, but trotted off on seeing us. Their sharp noses serve them well. A year later, in the Andaman Islands, we saw the remains of wild pig and water monitor feasts on turtle eggs.

A hundred and thirty seven eggs in all. Valli marked the spot with a stick after the mother turtle filled it with sand, so we could find them later. And then began the most incredible phase of the whole exercise. Lying on the now closed, flattened nest, Mrs Ridley proceeded to rock her forty kilogram body and shell from side to side in a comic sort of tap dance. The deep drumbeat sound she made blended with the booming surf. Having packed in her eggs, she proceeded to make a false nest, rotating round and vaguely agitating the sand with her flippers while moving away from the nest site. Ten minutes later she made her way to the water's edge again and we watched the domed figure enter the surf, disappear, surface again until finally she was gone, bound for an unknown destination. The only job that remained was for us to haul the eggs back to the hatchery. On some nights when we found too many eggs to carry we would rub out tracks, probably one of the simplest ways of protecting these turtles.

Two months and many nests later Jean Delouche was at our doorstep at the crack of dawn, looking a little worn. 'Hey! All night I've been listening to those damned turtles of yours! Keech-keech-keech all night long. *Alors* — the whole rotten bunch is hatching at once'.

We went back with him to find that half the 'rotten bunch' had hatched and the fenced in hatchery was dotted with black shapes grappling weakly with the sand. The initial twenty four hours of a sea turtle's life are crucial and survival requires determined effort on its part. It has to break free of the egg shell with the help of the tiny egg tooth, then scramble frantically to get out of the nest hole. The simultaneous activity of its hundred siblings creates an upward movement towards light and freedom. In the frantic melee, some usually suffocate to death. This same scrambling instinct has to carry the babies quickly past the menace of predators, first on the beach and then in the sea, and also helps them through the powerful waves and currents.

Rom managed to popularize these turtle walks among school and college students and to make them regular programmes organized by the WWF. At the time this was being enthusiastically looked after by Anne Joseph, the Snake Park's secretary for several years. Walking along the beach stretches within the city limits sometimes brought added excitement, and two or three times groups were held up at knife point and had to surrender watches, money and jewellery. We ourselves had a close encounter one night. We were out with the German film maker, Heinz Kramer and his wife, who wanted to film the nesting sequence of the Ridley. Kramer was deeply stricken by the plight of the exploited sea turtle and when we came across two egg collectors forging onward with bags of eggs, he could not control his anger and brandished a pocket knife at them. *'Schweinhund!'* he thundered. And, turning to the other man, *'Schweinhund. Das darf man nicht! Nicht erlaubt. Schweinhund!'* The egg collectors shouted with fear and fishermen from a nearby village came running to their defence. Realizing he'd got a tiger by the tail, Herr Kramer pocketed his knife; but it was difficult convincing his enemies

Like a few other turtles in the world, the male painted Kachuga dons brilliant colours in the breeding season. This is a turtle of the Ganges which often appears in the meat markets.

that the little murder threat had been a mistake, and for a while it looked tricky.

A few days after this incident we were back on the beach with the Kramers, edging along the hard sand at the water's margin in a hired jeep packed with filming equipment, including a generator for the flood lights, tripods, cameras. They did manage to film a nesting female Ridley, but then the jeep gave a sudden cough and froze, as the advancing tide lapped greedily at the wheels. Half an hour later the water was considerably higher and we were just beginning to unload the equipment and consign the vehicle to the deep when the engine suddenly came to life once more.

Rom was writing in all directions about the plight of sea turtles in India and together with Valli wrote a booklet on the olive Ridley of the Coromandel Coast that was printed and distributed by the Snake Park. All this publicity helped and when the Wildlife Protection Act of 1972 was formulated, the five species of sea turtles which are found in Indian waters, the Ridley, green, loggerhead, hawksbill and leatherback were included in its first Schedule. Penalties for collecting eggs and killing turtles could include heavy fines and even jail sentences. On paper, the sea turtles were very well off; but typically, the detailed laws had little relation to the reality in the field.

In spite of the laws there were still regular markets, mainly along the east coast, where turtles were openly slaughtered; in Calcutta several thousand Ridleys came to the markets every year from Orissa. On the Tamil Nadu coast, small fish markets often had a few sea turtles too, but at Tuticorin it was a weekly affair and on Sunday mornings fishermen brought in their week's catch of turtles to butcher. To verify reports of the continuing trade our secretary Anne Joseph, Binod Choudhury of the Government's crocodile project and I took the overnight bus to Tuticorin and walked down to the market at dawn to photograph the illegal butchering. It was a sight to turn the strongest stomach. Soon after our arrival, upturned turtles started coming in wheelbarrows and three-wheel tempos. During the two hours we were there, over thirty sea turtles, Ridleys, greens and hawksbills were brought in. Then the butchers took over. The plastron or lower shell of the living turtle was prised open and the insides removed as the flippers beat frantically in mad agony. Soon there were piles of intestines and meat, still twitching and jerking. Mouths gulped for air in non existent lungs, eyes on severed heads blinked slowly.

When the turtles were first cut up the blood drinkers would queue up carrying their small stainless steel cups and bowls; mostly old people hoping to revive their waning powers through the age old elixir. It cost a rupee per cup and the fresh blood had to be drunk quickly, in one gulp, before it congealed. A year later the government of Tamil Nadu received a strange petition from the Sea Turtle Blood Drinker's Association of Tuticorin, asking permission to continue their traditional activities in the interests of their health!

A few days before our visit there had been one of the periodical cases of poisoning from eating the meat of the hawksbill, a phenomenon that occurs now and then but which has not been satisfactorily explained. The Sri Lankan herpetologist Deraniyagala, reported in 1939 that the hawksbill is rendered poisonous after it feeds on certain algae. "Experienced fishermen" he wrote, "seldom eat an *Eretmochelys* without first chopping up its raw liver and throwing it to the crows. If the latter discard the liver, the animal is poisonous...".

One of the best things that has happened to sea turtles in India is Satish Bhaskar who worked for Rom for four years, surveying nesting beaches and populations on mainland India and its offshore islands. At the time we first met Satish he was a student at the Indian Institute of Technology, but his schedule did not include the classroom; everyday, he'd jog to the beach two kilometres away, have a long swim, jog back and pore over books on sea shells and coral reefs. To break the monotony, he would sometimes have a swim in the evening too. When Rom offered him the job of mapping sea turtle nesting beaches and collecting data on their status and distribution, a slow ecstasy dawned on his sun beaten face. 'Wow', he said.

Knapsack on his back, Satish started walking. He covered over a thousand kilometres along the east and west coasts of India, timing his visits with the reported turtle nesting seasons in that area. Often he slept on the beach in a boat or on the sand, being persecuted by sand flies, village dogs (he was bitten once) and once, by a group of thugs. He combines a sort of hard burning energy in the field with accurate and readable reports and this combination has made him one of the ace field biologists in India today. Satish is now an internationally acknowledged sea turtle man and recently worked in Indonesia, formulating a management plan for the huge leatherback turtles there.

Unfortunately, while Rom and I were away in Papua New Guinea for two years from '78 to '80, Satish had an altercation with the group of trustees in charge of the Snake Park's administration, and resigned. Luckily, WWF, India asked him to continue his surveys for them and one of the first areas he looked at were the Lakshadweep Islands in the Arabian Sea, just west of the Kerala coast. He spent five months on the uninhabited Suheli Island during the monsoon to record the green turtle's nesting patterns there. There is no inter-island transport in Lakshadweep during the rains and a fishing boat dropped him at the island in early May promising to return in mid September. But the monsoon was prolonged and the boatman couldn't get permission to cross to Suheli until mid October, a delay which must have been an anxious one for Satish. On his departure from Madras we saw him off with comforting possibilities of what may be in store for him — what if you break an arm, a leg? Sea snake bite? Run out of freshwater? Appendicitis? As it happened his biggest problem turned out to be a ten metre whale shark which was washed up, dead and very rotten, on his beach and soon the entire island was enveloped with the stench. Fortunately, the sea finally relented, carrying away its smelly cargo once more.

By this time Satish was married to our secretary at the Snake Park, Brenda Leveiro and their first child, Nyla, was born a few weeks before Satish ventured forth on his dangerous island mission. Sitting in the solitude of Suheli, he wrote Brenda several letters, sealed them in bottles and consigned them to the ocean, asking the finder to forward them to Brenda. She got one of these letters, sent on by a Sri Lankan fisherman, five weeks after it was written.

Satish's major triumph during these surveys was in the beautiful Nicobar Islands where he found a rookery or mass nesting ground of the leatherback turtle, which grows to two metres in length and is the largest of the world's sea turtles. His letters were always full of adventure and discovery. "Met a shell diver who has encountered sharks on numerous occasions while diving and has seen a Bengali colleague dismembered off Herbertabad. When I questioned him about sharks, the first incident he related was about a codiver who grabbed his neck and hung on in terror when approached by a 'monster' — which was a dugong.

"At Cuthbert Bay, Middle Andaman, I found another leatherback excavation and inadvertently got to within a few inches of a sea snake once again. It was in ankle deep water, probably making for nearby rocks when I disturbed it and it made off after splashing me. Did no more shore walking that night and slept on a high rock! Soon after that, on Little Andaman, I saw my first nesting leather back. She had finished egg laying and was camouflaging the nest area when I saw her. Tried barring her path to the sea by standing in front of her but she kept coming on and I had to step aside."

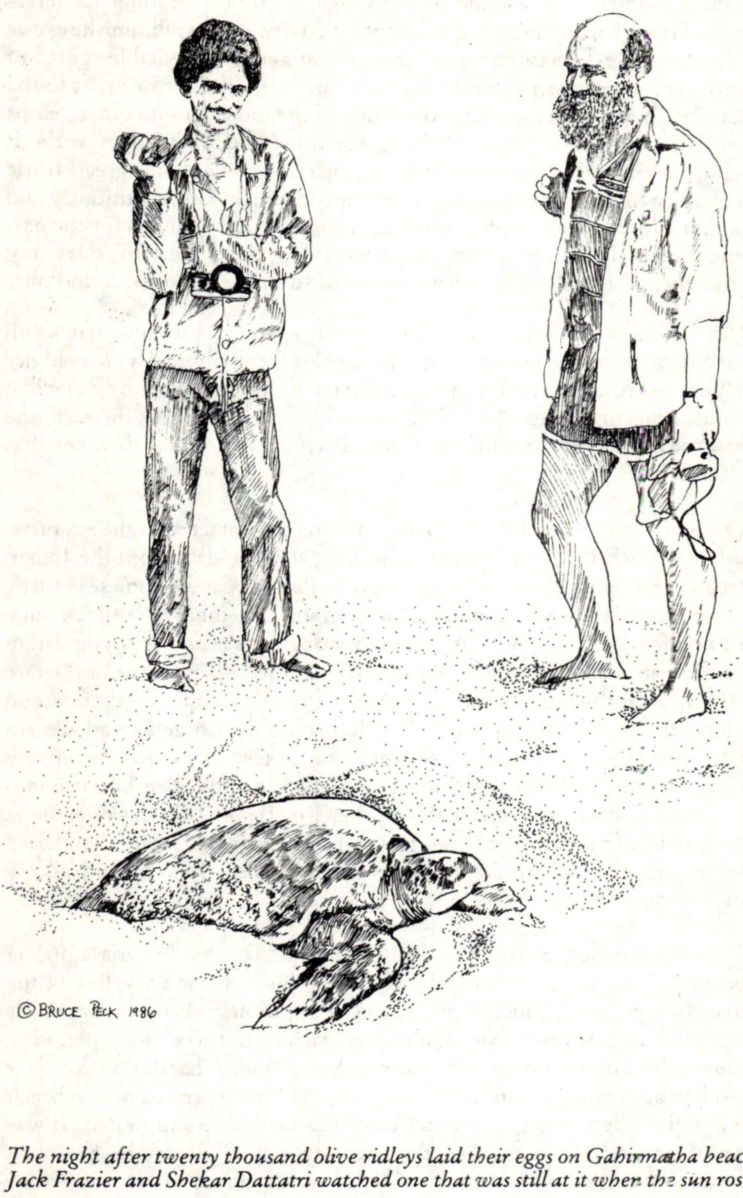

The night after twenty thousand olive ridleys laid their eggs on Gahirmatha beach, Jack Frazier and Shekar Dattatri watched one that was still at it when the sun rose.

Little Andaman is the home of the Onge, a group of hunter gatherers about whom hardly anything is known . They are fast diminishing due to the take over of large areas of their forest and the inevitable spread of the 'development disease' and drink that new comers have brought to the area. Satish was lucky enough to see one of the more remote Onge camps near West Bay. He'd been walking for three and a half days without seeing people. "I ran into a camp, occupants missing, and green turtle meat roasted and just begging to be eaten, which I surreptitiously did (being really famished — had eaten only biscuits and vitamins for the past four days). I left two biscuit packets for the Onge to salve my conscience... actually to reduce chances of stopping a spear if found out!

"Let me tell you what happened at Trinket Island. I'd found a hawksbill nest the previous night and tired after trekking the whole day, spread my polythene ground sheet on the beach. At 4 am I was woken by a rustling sound near my head. It was a crocodile gaping at me through the mosquito net. My enthusiasm for sleeping on sandy beaches has suffered".

Both Satish and Rom were fortunate in being in contact with the sea turtle biologist, Jack Frazier who has collected extensive data from the Indian Ocean and published an impressive pile of papers on sea turtle distribution, ecology and conservation. In the December of '84 Jack came to India for the Bombay Natural History Society's centenary symposium and thereafter spent a couple of months in Madras. Jack is one of the rare naturalists always open and generous with ideas and suggestions and willing to help others in the field. He managed to organize all the sea turtle nesting data for Madras from our notes, scattered over many exercise books and sheets of papers, and injected a lot of enthusiasm into the group of students associated with the Croc Bank. This was often done while swimming in the ocean in front of our home, his metre long beard floating in the waves. With his twinkling eyes, Jack looked like a mischevious octopus.

With Jack Frazier, Rom went to the Gahirmatha coast in Orissa during February '85, to see the annual *arribada* — Spanish for arrival — of the olive Ridleys. In this incredible nesting orgy, thousands upon thousands of sea turtles nest on the five kilometre beach over a week long period in January-February and again in April. Along with Chandra Shekar Kar who has been studying the *arribada* since 1977, they arrived on the beach on a night when twenty thousand turtles came ashore and nested. It was one of nature's frenzies, like the mass migration across the Serengeti plains. Wave upon wave of them hobbled out of the sea to nest and return to the ocean as if taking part in some bizzare military operation. There was not enough space on the beach for all the nests, so females were digging up other nests. Egg yolk and sticky sand flew in all directions.

Rom wrote that "the hours went by quickly as the flow of turtles seemed to ebb and swell with its own dynamic tide. This was a small *arribada* but that did not detract from the excitement as we pondered over the mechanisms and senses that caused the turtles to travel in huge flotillas which coast guard officers once described as 'islands of turtles migrating northward'. Over two million eggs were laid that night and over forty million in the season".

Just as it is virtually impossible to count the number of turtles coming up during an *arribada*, it is even more difficult to predict how many hatchlings make it back to the sea after their fifty to sixty day incubation under the sand. Wild boar, hyenas, jackals, lizards, cats, crabs and birds prey on the eggs and the successive waves of nesting females destroy millions. No wonder it is estimated that after a year of hazards as few as one in a thousand may survive.

In 1981 Chandra Shekar discovered another *arribada* beach with a hundred thousand nesters on two or three kilometres of beach. It now appears that over half a million female Ridleys use the Orissa rookeries.

In late March and early April the beach is again dark with moving shapes. Millions of tiny hatchlings crawl laboriously through a deadly gauntlet of crabs and birds. Only fifteen grams in weight compared to their forty kilogram mothers, the little turtles instinctively head towards the sea, attracted by the glow of the waves and reflection of the stars. Meanwhile, nature pulls one of its dark jokes and a new *arribada* of adult females starts in the midst of hatching. The care one takes not to step on the hatchlings is made a mockery of by the adults who just clamber over the babies, suffocating them under their heavy plastrons by the thousands.

Jack Frazier and Rom spent a lot of time discussing the future of this massive breeding population of turtles. Will its fragile habitat, buffeted by annual cyclones, survive? Should one persist with total preservation and not acknowledge the resource potential? Can a number of turtles or eggs be safely taken to supply the massive demand in West Bengal? If so, how do we arrive at figures and a system that will prevent over exploitation? There are some ill advised efforts to attempt captive breeding of Ridleys in India instead of concentrating research effort and money on the wild population. Captive rearing of turtles in Orissa which has the largest wild nesting populations of Ridleys in the world and where neither the meat nor the eggs are eaten, would use up local protein in the form of shellfish, crabs, shrimp and fish which are eaten by the local people.

A few days before Rom and Jack arrived at Gahirmatha, the Chief Minister of Orissa landed on the beach in a helicopter to see the sea turtles. Governmental sympathy and concern for the survival of the Ridleys began in 1976 when the Forest Department banned the lifting of eggs from Gahirmatha. But poaching continued unabated and Chandra Shekar watched poachers just offshore, hauling the helpless animals into their boats as they returned from nesting, with their tags that he had clipped on. The catch was transferred to trawlers and ended up at Howrah station in Calcutta. In 1982, *India Today* published photographs of the mass poaching taken by J Vijaya, one of Rom's assistants, and this led to an outcry, highlighted by a letter campaign from the international sea turtle conservationists, to the Prime Minister. Mrs Gandhi acted quickly and decisively and the following year navy and coast guard ships patrolled the sea when nesting began. Helicopters, fixed wing aircraft and patrol boats apprehended poachers as the turtles nested with a massive protection force looking on. In another enlightened move, the Orissa government banned the use, during the nesting season, of the deadly offshore trawlers in which turtles are often trapped and drowned.

The future of sea turtles in India is uncertain. The danger, as always, comes from uncontrolled trade and not from the local consumption of meat. In the Andaman and Nicobar Islands the tribes and local settlers have speared turtles for generations and this has remained a sustained source of protein for a small number of people; but when organised business interests set in then there is little chance of the populations holding out. The Central Government now has a sea turtle specialist group — of which Rom and Satish Bhaskar are members — but research has been meagre and repetitious and efforts in the field insufficient. Help for sea turtles must go beyond seminars and legislation.

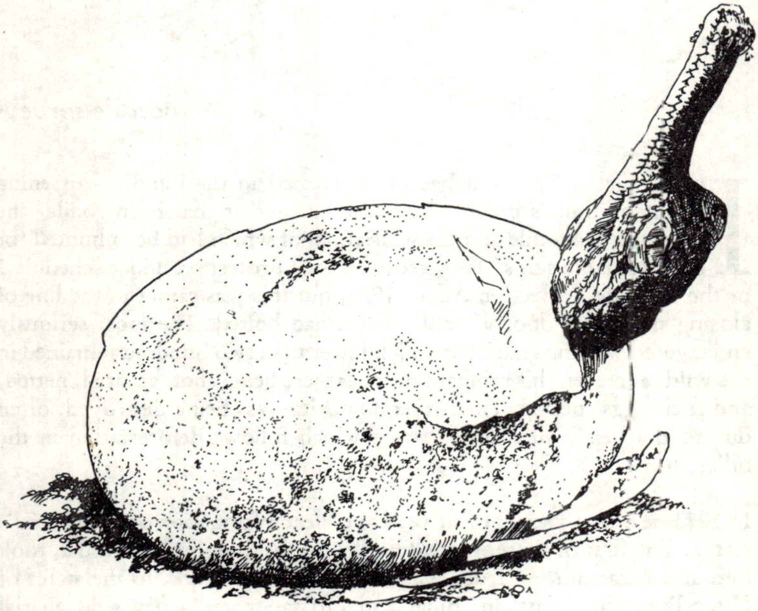

A baby gharial takes its first peep at the world.

crocodile surveys

In the early '70s, Rom became interested in the rapidly worsening plight of India's crocodilians: the mugger or marsh crocodile, the saltwater crocodile and the gharial, all of which had been hunted for their valuable skins. They received total protection under schedule 1 of the Wildlife Protection Act of 1972, but this was rather in the line of closing the stable door after the horse had bolted. The most seriously endangered was the gharial of which fewer than two hundred remained in the wild; and even this remnant number were being shot, speared, netted, and their eggs robbed. Their riverine habitat was being destroyed, often due to the heavy siltation of rivers which follows deforestation in the hills.

In 1973 he began a series of surveys to collect information on the gharial's status. The first of these, funded by World Wildlife Fund — India, took him and Rajamani, an Irula assistant at the Snake Park, to the states of Uttar Pradesh, Rajasthan, Bihar and Orissa, where a few wild gharial reportedly survived in stretches of the Ganges, Chambal and Mahanadi rivers. Shikar tales from the turn of the century told of rivers teeming with both mugger and gharial, and reports of over twenty gharial on one sandbank were common. But now the picture was totally different.

Weighing just a hundred grams on its hatchday, this baby saltwater crocodile could grow to a length of seven metres and increase to a thousand kilogrammes in weight.

By the end of a three month journey they had collected a lot of bad news and run out of money. The Snake Park sent a money order to the general post office in Cuttack, Orissa, but the postmaster wouldn't allow Rom to collect it without an identity card, and the local police station understandably refused to issue one. 'How are we to know you are you', the postmaster insisted, until they gave up.

At the time they were eight hundred kilometres from Madras, with seven rupees on them, no place to stay and no friends. Rom thought it would be too embarassing to approach the Raja of Kanika, whom they had just met, so they tried another strategy. Putting on khaki shirts after washing up at the railway station they strode into the Circuit House. 'Crocodile officers from the Madras Snake Park', announced Rom at the reception and procured a room, coffee and lunch.

The choice was now between thumbing a ride south or attempting ticketless train travel. Rajamani favoured the former. By then he was disgusted with the northern cold and the wheat diet which he said was very weakening to his rice accustomed system. 'The last thing we need is to get arrested by a ticket inspector', he groaned.

The next morning they were at the south bound highway at dawn, holding a placard saying "Madras". As luck would have it, a truck slowed down soon after and fifty hours later its driver Ram Singh dropped them at the gate of the Snake Park. During the journey he supplied them with tea, food and smokes, feeling intensely sorry for the white sahib who had fallen on bad times. Sitting on top of Ram Singh's truck, Rom wrote me a letter about his future plans for crocodiles. "Tell your father I am making out a proposal to hit WWF for money to start a crocodile breeding farm. Captive breeding is the only thing that will save them, there is too much pressure on wild populations. A croc farm might even provide us with a 'living', which the Snake Park certainly won't do. I would like Mrs Whitaker to have three meals a day, though it does seem slightly ambitious...."

A year later the New York Zoological Society sponsored further surveys and a friend of Rom's, E Mahadev, mapped in the missing links in Madhya Pradesh, Arunachal Pradesh and Assam, travelling on his motorbike with a bedroll strapped to the pillion. His conclusion was that large net fishing, shooting and the damming of rivers had accelerated the gharial's decline.

In 1974, Andy Ross of the Smithsonian Institution came to Corbett National Park to observe the gharial and mugger on the Ramganga River.

Rom and his Snake Park colleague, D Basu decided to go with him and the three of them spent six weeks watching the crocodiles of the area and interviewing local fishermen about their previous and present status. They found two pools which were frequently used by five gharial and eight mugger and constructed rough blinds from where they could watch the activity on the river.

One afternoon in May, Rom was sitting in one of the blinds over-looking the gharial pool, dozing off periodically. It was hot and sticky, rain not far away. Just as the first sounds of thunder rolled down the valley Basu and he decided to call it a day and walked to the Gairal rest house, to find Andy, who had seen a large three metre mugger from a few paces away. They went back with him and there was the croc just lying on the bank, only hissing as they moved closer and closer. He was obviously very sick, his body covered with wounds, possibly from homemade bombs of black powder and plaster of Paris which woodcutters used to bomb fish in the deep pools.

The mugger died soon after and Andy Ross, a rabid taxonomist, decided that the skeleton must be saved for a museum collection. Whole mugger specimens are scarce, he declared, adding that since they only had a couple of days left, burying the skeleton was impossible. It may take three weeks for the bones to get completely free of rotten meat and gristle underground. So after the vultures had a full day's feast, the three of them — Andy, Rom and Basu — worked with handkerchiefs tied over their noses and half hourly tots of local brew to help bear the horrible stench. They worked at night to avoid the flies. The skeleton now resides at the Kukkrail Crocodile Centre.

Often they walked eighteen kilometres down river to the main rest house at Dikhala. One afternoon they saw a large croc slide into a side pool on a dry tributary or 'sot'. Basu, who had a bad cold, stretched out on the path adjoining the jungle's edge. Andy walked up the dry tributary and Rom sat waiting with his camera to see if the croc came up again. After a while he saw Andy coming back down and so started towards Basu who was about a hundred metres round a bend. Suddenly, a tiger came out of the jungle on the other side of the tributary directly in front of him, making a fantastic orange collage against the white river stones. It coughed once and didn't see Rom until the latter had whistled sharply to Andy. The tiger was heading straight down the path where Basu was sleeping. So they shouted 'Basu, tiger!' and started racing towards him; but the tiger leaped up the rocks and cliffs, disappearing over the hill.

Basu looked up and sleepily enquired what the commotion was all about. 'Nothing much, just that a tiger almost ran over you'. That was not Basu's day; later on in the afternoon, a kilometre from Dikhala, Andy and Rom were ahead and saw a big tusker stride out from the forest and come towards them. They started walking swiftly to get well ahead of where he was going to cross the road, looking back to get Basu's attention just in time. He started to sprint, but by now the tusker had got to the forests' edge near the road. They yelled for Basu to stop, which he did, slowly crouching against a tree and trying to look small. The elephant stood still, one foot raised in doubt, then crossed over slowly.

Often bumping into elephants, they criss-crossed Corbett which seemed increasingly small and vulnerable: just six kilometres upriver were villages and farmlands, and on the regular riverside path, tiger pugs, deer and human tracks obliterated each other. It was not all hot slogging in the sun; Rom indulged in his passion for fishing using a hand line and bread dough, and often returned to the rest house with hefty mahseer and bleeding cuts from the line.

They walked the length of the Ramganga in the Park by day and later by night. Porcupines were some of their common companions on nocturnal walks along the river and one evening they found the answer to the old question of how porcupines mate: with extreme care. They would sit on a bluff overlooking Boksar, once a well known gharial spot, and watch the water backing up river from the Kalagarh Dam, of which the last spillway had been closed. Deforestation in the lower Himalaya has created a situation which ensures devastating run-off, erosion and floods down below on the plains with every monsoon. Authorities often use this argument to justify the construction of dams. But unfortunately migratory animals, like the great mahseer fish, the unique riverine gharial and the Gangetic dolphin are never considered when these developments take place. The real answer of course is tree planting and stopping further deforestation, which are only now being considered important.

These surveys also turned up information on the ecology and behaviour of wild crocodiles, a subject largely unexplored except for a few fragmentary notes in journals. In '75, for instance, Rom was censusing crocodiles in Gujarat and spent a week in the Barda Hills in Kutch. It was the worst drought in forty years and over fifty mugger were reported to have been killed while trekking overland looking for water. Rom followed one track a kilometre up into the scrub jungle hills, to find — and catch — a metre and a half mugger lying half hidden under a large boulder. It was in search of water, possibly on its way to a reservoir twelve kilometres away.

Another strategy that mugger use to tide over the hot season is to dig tunnels. These are usually from about three to six metres deep and a metre in diameter. They are often horizontal and sometimes horseshoe shaped, with two entrances. Mugger that live in hill streams and in the small rivers such as the Hiran river in Gir, which often dry up leaving only large, deep, perennial pools, use tunnels all year long. Rom was with Jeevan Nana, a Maldhari living in the Gir while searching around Hiran Lake looking for croc nests. They found eighteen tunnels dug into the embankments of the then almost dry lake.

He and Jeevan were on a steep cliff — so steep that you couldn't imagine a mugger climbing up; but there were ascending tracks from the water and Rom peered down to investigate. As he bent over the cliff's edge, there, half a metre from his face, were the jaws of a large mugger flush with the embankment.

While this was the first detailed look at the crocodiles in Gujarat, Rom had already conducted fairly thorough surveys in his home state of Tamil Nadu on the status of the only species found there, the mugger or marsh crocodile. This adaptable croc was once common in rivers, lakes, streams and any habitat with a bit of water and protection. But now Gujarat and Tamil Nadu seemed to have the largest populations, the latter with about two hundred and fifty animals living in nine or ten habitats scattered throughout the state. Even so, in '74, two years after the implementation of the Wildlife Act, one of the Snake Park's volunteers stood by with open mouth as a mugger caught on a baited hook in the Cauvery river was tied up and carried away to be skinned. The clandestine profits from one such skin is worth several months pay to a fisherman or rural labourer, which makes effective law enforcement difficult indeed.

Rom saw that there was a need for urgent action on someone's part, if crocodiles were to be saved from extinction in India. Not only were they being killed for their skins, but almost all the eggs were collected during the nesting season, February to May in the south, to be turned into omelettes. His lifelong fascination for dinosaurs perhaps motivated him to try and save these hundred million year old creatures. It was difficult to stomach the idea of such powerful, dramatic predators fading away from their rightful Indian habitat. But what could he do? Finally, he wrote up a proposal to collect eggs from wild nests in Tamil Nadu, incubate and hatch them at the Snake Park and hand over a percentage to the Forest Department after rearing them for a year. The Chief

The strange, forest lizard of the hills of central Sri Lanka. It opens its mouth wide when threatened and has earned the local name of 'devil lizard'.

Conservator of Forests agreed but in the first year Rom got to the main habitat, Amaravati, to find eleven empty nest holes baking in the sunlight.

The answer was to plant nest guards from the Snake Park at the major nesting locations, well ahead of the start of the season and thus raise the egg catch by several notches. 1975 saw the first experiment along these lines and it was a success. With Mahadev, Solomon (Snake Park assistant) and our Irula friend Chockalingam, we drove south to Chidambaram and on through to Vakkaramari Waterworks which then had a population of twenty mugger. Our Himalayan war surplus Nissan Jonga had its first, and one of many, tantrums just south of Chinglepet. 'Brakes failed', Rom announced calmly as we slid rapidly towards a ditch after narrowly missing a bullock cart. That was half a day's delay while a mechanic was brought and proceeded to repair the severed brake line.

At Chidambaram Natesan, the nest guard stationed there, had good news for us. The previous day he had almost stumbled over a mugger nesting in broad daylight on one of the bunds dividing the two main tanks. 'Let's get the eggs now, those mongooses have been nosing about near the nest.' Dirty and tired, we set about unpacking the plywood boxes in which the eggs would be safe on their journey to Madras. Fifty centimetres square and twenty centimetres deep with perforations for air, we lined one of these with slightly damp earth and in the orange glow of dusk, transferred the white oblong shapes to their foster nest. The female watched from the water's edge five metres away as the earth was scraped back and each egg lifted carefully out without turning it. The top was marked with a cross and placed in the box in exactly the same position. Turning or jarring an egg could rupture the delicate blood vessels attaching the embryo to the shell wall. 'Handle them like nitroglycerine', Rom advised Mahadev, 'and they'll make it'.

Each layer of eggs was covered with earth and humus to make them as shock proof as possible and the box deposited in a corner of the Waterwork's office. It would be Natesan's job to keep the eggs damp and free from ants until half the sixty day incubation period was over, when he could take them back to Madras by train with a minimum of worry about damaging the by then strong embryos. Exhausted, we rolled up on the ground in sleeping bags after a dinner of glucose biscuits and bananas.

Early next morning we loaded up for the three hundred and seventy five kilometre drive to Amaravati Reservoir, now part of the Annamalais Wildlife Sanctuary which is one of the last refuges of the Nilgiri tahr. The reservoir itself is a standing example of how natural fish predators like crocodiles can actually be beneficial to the fisheries industry. The mugger at Amaravati feed on catfish, cormorants, otters, turtles and a number of other creatures which in turn hunt the commercially valuable species of fish. Of course, you cannot tell a fisherman this; for him, crocs break nets and eat fish, and that's that. But the fact that Amaravati has both the highest fish catch in India as well as the largest southern population of crocodiles is more than just a coincidence.

Nesting hadn't begun at Amaravati. All we could see were faint trial nests and a lot of tracks zig-zagging across the banks, which indicated that the females were active: egg laying would start any day. There was also a lot of disturbance along the lake shore. Fishermen and cow herders with their herds of cattle had driven up towards good grazing areas. At night the wild creatures took over, with elephants and sambar coming down from the hills for a drink. We wondered if the increased daytime activity on the banks had disturbed the nesting schedules of the mugger — or maybe they were nesting elsewhere! A year later, walking around Amaravati with our friend Binod Choudhary, one of the government's crocodile conservation officers, we saw a strange phenomenon. Following tracks leading out of the water we came upon a three metre female, a kilometre from the water's edge. She had clambered halfway up a small hill, over rocks and thorny bushes, and later laid her eggs in these inhospitable surroundings; but the soil was not deep enough for a nest and the eggs rolled down the dry hillside and broke.

We left Solomon in Amaravati to collect the eggs before the poachers got them. Before going on to the next habitat, Bhavani Sagar, we spent a night out on the reservoir 'shining' for croc eyes from one of the locally popular coracles. These circular boats, nearly two metres in diameter, are made from buffalo hides stitched together with leather. The frame is bamboo, woven like a basket. Twenty pairs of gleaming orange eyes answered our spotlight beam. Without quite knowing what he was doing, our boatman got us within a few metres of the granddaddy, a four metre giant who was lying on a slab of rock facing us. The flimsy coracle oared silently up to the dreaming crocodile, all of us expecting him to retreat, but he didn't; and we realized how vulnerable the coracle or parasal could be. When we were practically on him there was a massive splash and the boat rocked as he dived under us and shot away. We could feel his bumpy back scrape the underside of the coracle.

Talking of coracles, a year later we were at Sathanur Dam closer to Madras being given a coracle tour by Kalimuthu, one of the local fishermen, when a sudden squall blew up on the reservoir. The intensity of the wind whipping up the waves was frightening and our fisherman friend glanced apprehensively at the water sloshing over the sides of the boat. Rom bailed with a coconut shell and Kalimuthu took us towards the shore with strong paddle strokes. Knowing how difficult it is to keep one of these coracles going in a straight line even in calm waters, I was amazed at this fisherman's skill. We reached the shore just in time because a huge storm was following at the heels of the wind and hailstones suddenly started falling. But Kalimuthu was prepared for any weather. He hauled the coracle up on the pebbly bank, turned it over, bottom facing the wind. We all crawled underneath, dry and with a nice view of the storm on the lake.

But to go back to Amaravati, we left the next morning for Bhavani Sagar Dam, which is flanked by the Nilgiris, the Blue Mountains. At the dam itself there was just one trial nest hole; but the rest house cook at Bhavani town told us of a small group of mugger living in Kedarhalla stream four hundred metres up in the Nilgiri foothills, on the Kerala border. This was exciting news indeed; it was the first report of mugger still surviving in a wild, unaltered habitat in Tamil Nadu. So far all the mugger we had seen were in manmade environments, reservoirs and tanks. The best time to survey the stream would be at night, and we decided to go the next day and camp on the bank. Mahadev and I went out and bought provisions - rice, dal, tea, sugar - and tried to find a guide to take us up to the stream. But this last proved impossible; the Kedarhalla area was haunted and no one was prepared to come, certainly not for the night. We finally set off on our own and picked up the watchman of the Electricity Board at Gejeleti village, on the banks of the Moyar River at an exhorbitant price. The next day half way up the hill, he doubled his fee with cunning presence of mind.

In the morning the sun rose like a red hot piece of coal; the gentle interval between night and day had been done away with, and this was summer in earnest. The track which led to Gejeleti village below the croc pools was like an obstacle race, and the Jonga bulldozed its way through the patches of scrub, between large boulders and down steep dry stream beds. Further on, we stopped at a cattle camp which had been ravaged by elephants the night before; the feeble thorn fences were torn down, banana trees stripped, two huts trampled and practically shredded. Over the last two years three people had been killed by elephants in this area, all of which pointed to the dramatic dwindling of forest habitat in south India and the increased harassment by ivory poachers. A forest official in Bhavani had told us that elephant poachers were now hanging live wires from electric lines and the trauma and slow death of the animals was unimaginable. Forest Department officials had recovered several carcasses after the painful device finally killed them. Today, elephant poaching has reached frightening dimensions and it looks like the south Indian tusker may be on the way out.

On the drive up towards the Moyar river we saw several small herds of elephants dotting the dusty, dry hillsides and their tracks on the banks. They were sticking close to the river this time of year but it was incongruous to see the big animals in the dry, low thorn forest. Here we almost had to turn back, not because of the jumbos but because the flood gates had been opened and the Moyar, which flows into the Bhavani Sagar reservoir along with the Bhavani, was in spate. We decided to drive across anyway; twenty metres of white, surging water, a metre deep in some places. 'Motor no, motor no', pleaded the guide, which perversely was an added encouragement. In the event we almost lost the vehicle, and Rom as well. The Jonga lurched drunkenly across the furious water, once hitting a large boulder-dong/ and almost keeling over. As it reached the opposte bank with a final ponderous wobble Mahadev and I set up a strangled cheer.

Across the river there was not even a pretence of a track and Mahadev walked ahead, waving us cheerfully on over boulders and steep slopes, and the Jonga gave of its best. We parked the vehicle on the bank of the Kedarhalla stream, opposite a small *Kali* temple which, our guide explained, a tiger visits every year at Dussehra to watch the people who come to make offerings and to pray. Suddenly, in mid story, he jerked his thumb disapprovingly at me. 'Women cannot go beyond this point. If she goes any further the *sami,* God, will get angry, and bring trouble for my family'. We tried to reason that any trouble would surely fall on me, not him, but he refused to accept this argument. Finally, the religious controversy was settled with a little sum of money, and we picked up our gear and started upstream towards the three pools which the watchman at Bhavani had described.

Two kilometres along the jungle's edge, at the beginning of a steep gorge before the first pool, we found a good place to camp, with large flat 'sleeping rocks' and plenty of shade. But the still stagnant water was filthy with slime, and undrinkable. We boiled some and scraped off the green layer hoping it was okay; but two days later I was so sick with dysentery that I had to be practically carried down to the Jonga. It was now getting dark and Chockalingam and I made a small fire and cooked up a tortured mess of rice, soup cubes and dal. After nightfall we 'shone'

A horned lizard was one of the several endemic Sri Lankan reptiles we came across.

Pool I for croc eyes, but saw nothing bigger than frogs and toads. On towards Pool 2, hopping along the big boulders on the banks as silently as possible. A young python was enjoying the retained heat of a large rock and almost got stepped on. It was so quiet in the forest, the birds and animals seemed to be holding their breath:but as we went further up into the box canyon there was a loud mysterious crash from overhead and all of us jumped in unison.

We 'shone' pool 2-nothing - and went on to Pool 3, the largest and deepest of the three. The guide, Chockalingam and I stopped fifty metres away, and Rom and Mahadev crept forward quietly to try and take the crocs by surprise. The pools had obviously been hunted recently and the crocs were sure to be wary and shy, going underwater at the least sign of danger. They can stay under for at least an hour, a factor which makes accurate censusing very difficult. Slowing down their heart beat, crocodiles are even known to stay underwater for several hours without coming up for a breath. They are able to do this through a physiological trick known as bradycardia when the heart beats go down to a beat per minute and the metabolic rate is almost suspended.

As Rom and Mahadev went ahead, we sat down to wait. Suddenly an agonized scream shattered our wits. 'Hari Ram', the guide whispered, trembling. Chockalingam and I froze, my body felt as if filled with iced water. It was several seconds before Rom came stumbling back in the dark, giving us another fright, to say it was the cry of the forest eagle owl which Samuel Baker in 1855 described as a "dull low note of indescribable pain and suffering". Having delivered this very comforting lecture he ran back to Pool 3 and returned half and hour later with Mahadev to announce two pairs of eyes, which had submerged as soon as the torch was clicked on, then surfaced for a few seconds fifteen minutes later. Back at Pool 1 and a couple of hours later, we craned over a rock to see two orange eyes floating near the edge of the bank. A total of three crocs; half the population from the previous year.

Just before dawn next day we collected around the breakfast pot. 'Continental menu', Mahadev grinned, less than eagerly, mixing his share of boiled *ragi*. 'Instant energy' — alternately taking mouthfuls and flexing his muscles. Walking back to Pool 1, Chockalingam found some tracks near the bank which led to a trial nest hole. Further on, another cavity with pieces of egg shell scattered on the ground and a dead hatchling on a nearby rock. Against all odds, the little mugger group of Kedarhalla was carrying out its tasks of procreation. The mother croc had carried the hatched and partly hatched young to the water, but there was no sign of them, so we decided to stay on another day to try and locate them. At this point our guide suddenly remembered some urgent work at home and disappeared, hoping to find a cowherd who would accompany him down to the plains.

I was cleaning my foot with spit in order to pull out a *babul* thorn when Rom nudged me energetically, pointing to a patch of sunlight on the water below a large rock outcrop. 'See that - there. Right there - see?' I couldn't see anything. 'Where, what?' I began but by then Rom was taking off his jeans and shirt and was in the water, gesturing to Chockalingam. Only then did I spot the knot of heads of about twenty hatchlings, floating vertically like little sticks in the shade of the large rock. By now Chockalingam with a *lungi,* was in the water too, and the two of them slowly waded and swam towards the group of tiny crocodiles, *lungi* spread like a fishing net beneath the surface.

It was a foolish but successful exercise. They were in three metres of murky, opaque water, at the mercy of a protective mother croc. After endless minutes the *lungi* was spread out in slow motion under the hatchlings and lifted up slowly. Nineteen baby crocs took their cue; we held our breaths as the chorus of wah, wah, wah filled the air. But the mother remained submerged; as often happens in heavily hunted areas, the natural defensive instincts were subdued by the fear of man. The babies were transferred to a box lined with leaves and earth, watered down and left at the camp site. We moved on upstream.

Pool 2, so normal in our torchbeams the night before, looked like a disaster area. Pieces of the poisonous euphorbia plant which deoxygenates water and is used as the local version of dynamite fishing, floated on the surface along with hundreds of dead fish. At one corner of the pool was a trickle of fresh water from upstream and to this the still living fish converged, mouths open, trying to breathe. The culprit, probably a cowherd from a neighbouring *patti,* had destroyed hundreds of valuable fish to get perhaps a dozen for his family.

Now Rom whistled from the other side of the pool. He was standing next to a slight mound of damp earth; a mugger nest, still intact. The raised dome looked untypical of the mugger, more like the nest of a saltwater crocodile. Closer, we noticed that the surface was very wet, almost as if a bucket of water had been recently poured over it. We guessed that the female crocodile evacuated water from her cloaca on to her nest. Rom kneeled down and tapped the earth covering with his fingers. Incredible: the unmistakable umph, umph of ready-to-hatch crocodiles. The faint protesting sounds are the vocal cue for the female crocodile to come and scrape the earth away so that the hatchlings can emerge. Standing in for her we dug down to the twenty five eggs and watched the young break free of their shells with varying degrees of energy. The first one out scrambled away from the nest hole and towards the water with a piece of egg shell worn rakishly over its head.

Crocodile survey and management projects eventually took Rom to many parts of the world including Africa, Bangladesh, Malaysia and Papua New Guinea for organisations interested in crocodile conservation or commercial farming possibilities, such as the World Wildlife Fund and the Food and Agriculture Organisation. Our experiences in these fascinating areas are too extensive to be a part of this book, but here's a description of the Sri Lanka survey of 1977, which Rom and I undertook at the invitation of the Wildlife and Nature Protection Society of Sri Lanka. Our job was to travel around the island identifying crocodile habitats, and to produce a report on the status and distribution of the two species found there, saltwater and mugger.

In order to be free from the uncertainties of public transport services, we took Rom's old Jawa motorcycle with us on the ferry from Rameswaram to Talaimannar in Sri Lanka; and over the two month survey period the old antique covered three thousand kilometres without as much as a puncture. The packing arrangements were a little painful, with me wedged between camera bags and knapsack at a marked slant, so that standing upright after a longish drive was difficult. Arriving at the port town of Talaimannar on the boat, we drove down to Colombo the next day just as the first showers of the northeast monsoon hit the south eastern corner of the island. With the help of our friend Ranil Senanayake, we made up data charts for the rivers and reservoirs which included salinity levels, night 'eye counts', vegetation. The most productive crocodile habitat, which in our report we recommended should be declared a crocodile sanctuary, was a lake called Panama near Arugam Bay in the south east. How well I remember weaving our way down that dirt track hung with camera and binoculars and me clutching the big green knapsack for balance, while a group of local children split their sides laughing! But the indignity was worthwhile: there in the early morning sunlight were about fifteen large mugger basking complacently on the banks, and in the depths of the forested lake shore beyond our vision we heard them catching fish with loud claps of their jaws.

The close approach that these mugger allowed us was very untypical of the species in south India. The bolting range of an animal is a useful

When we arrived at Panama Wewa in southeast Sri Lanka it was mid-morning. The sun warmed the banks of the tank and crocodiles basked on all sides. It was a primeval scene that is rarely seen on the subcontinent.

indication of the degree of protection it enjoys in the field, and we found many instances of happy coexistence between crocodiles and people in areas which poachers had left alone. At Kataragama, pilgrims bathed in the river while mugger soaked in the sun on rocks twenty metres away. But in some areas the animals allowed only a three hundred metre approach and we found that the main culprits were nomadic fishing clans who travel around the country systematically netting, hooking and trapping crocodiles, mainly for the meat.

The most interesting encounter of the survey was not with crocodiles but with old Mothalay Peter, a toothless Burgher of Dutch descent who was one of the regular croc catchers in the 40's when it was legal. Even now, in his 60s, he would take on nuisance - croc catching jobs for the local government agent. He and his family sat with us under coconut trees in front of his house at Batticaloa and told us how they caught giant gourami fish by wading into abandoned croc tunnels. But then Peter amazed us with his tales of catching mugger in the same way. He'd spot an active croc tunnel, and then crawl into the half submerged slimy hole with a rope but no light. Feeling in front of him very gingerly he would contrive to slip the rope around the crocodile's body. Crocodiles, like most reptiles, are quite ticklish and a gentle prod will make one raise its body just enough to slip the rope under. Tying a secure knot on it Peter would back out of the tunnels which are like one way streets, and he and his stalwarts would haul on the rope, bring the croc to the tunnel's mouth and axe it to death.

One of Peter's favourite stories is about the crocodile who didn't want a rope around himself and forced his way out of the tunnel the only way he could, over Peter. The claw marks on Peter's back are a reminder of this adventure.

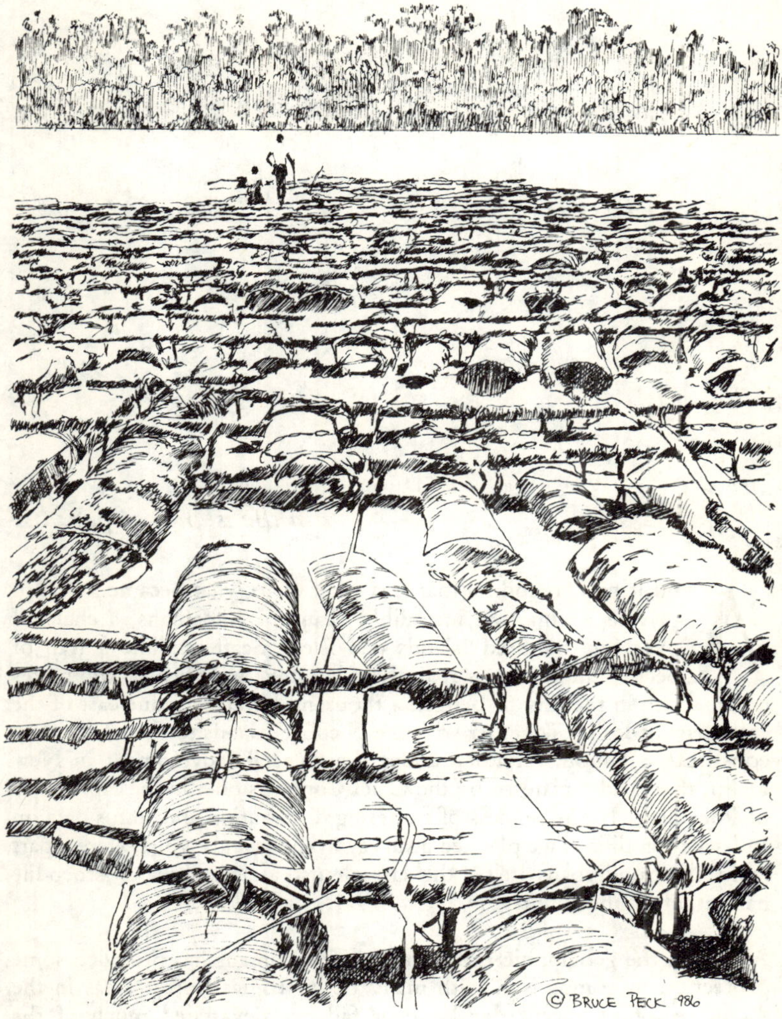

The Andaman forests are being devastated and the only way to transport the logs is by tying them together as rafts.

in the islands of paradise

And it was crocodiles that first took us to what became a sort of private Karma, the incredibly beautiful Andamans, a chain of over five hundred Islands and islets. Scattered like a trail of beetles these Islands span three hundred and seventy kilometres north-south in the Bay of Bengal, a thousand kilometres due east of the east coast of India. Together with the Nicobar Islands to the south, they constitute a Union Territory under the Central Government in New Delhi, that is administered by the Chief Commissioner in the capital city of Port Blair. In the process of gathering distribution and status data on India's crocodilians we planned a survey in the Islands which were, apart from the Sunderbans delta, the last almost intact saltwater crocodile habitat left in the country.

Although the geographic isolation of the Andamans has provided some protection in comparison with many other tropical forest areas in the Asian region, a recent development fad has devastated much of the pristine evergreen forest there. Authorised settlements and illegal land encroachments have had far reaching ecological effects. Practically every perennial freshwater stream has been colonized; the population has escalated to a staggering 400,000 (it was 50,000 in 1960); in the last twenty years two and a half million cubic metres of timber have been extracted, over a hundred thousand hectares of forest cleared and six hundred kilometres of road constructed. A lot of these developments are unplanned and disorganised, so that very often the powers-that-be are unaware of the realities. Several ecological impact teams have questioned the wisdom of these policies but so far with dismally small effect.

A year after our marriage, in '75, we tried to visit the Islands. But it proved impossible for Rom to do so, being an American citizen. Only a handful of foreigners had been allowed there since Independence, including King Leopold II of Belgium and the Italian anthropologist Lidio Cipriani, who did a classic study on the Onge tribals.

Rom had been reading and painstakingly collecting every reference he could find on the Andamans, one of the most interesting rain forests in south east Asia. It seemed trivial that a mere passport should come in the way of his going there and since he'd decided to live in India anyway, he applied to become an Indian citizen by naturalization. Family and friends cautioned him that this was a serious and irreversible decision, and I myself was in two minds about its wisdom. But Rom thought that being an Indian citizen would also make his overall conservation work easier.

Having filed his papers, the next step was to go to the American Consulate and hand in his passport. The Consul laid a fatherly hand on his shoulder and asked, 'Are you sure, Son, you're doing the right thing?' 'Sure do', answered Rom.

For a year thereafter he was stateless, and unable to travel at all. He asked if I would be prepared to go to the Islands on a feeler trip mainly to make contacts and gather whatever general information I could on the saltwater crocodile. The idea appealed. Our vanguard team comprised the then manager of the Snake Park, RK Menon, Irula assistant Annamalai and myself. That first six week sojourn was the beginning of a relationship with the Islands which borders on the passionate. The Islands hold many elements very special to us; the hostile tribal communities fighting for survival against the ever increasing dangers of development and shrinking territories, the jewel-like coral reefs dotting the deep blue sea, the thick tangle of evergreen forests fringed with beaches where sea turtles nest in the vast white expanse, and where sea snakes come up to lay their eggs in thousands.

On the deck of the INS State of Haryana on the way to Port Blair, I found a chair which achieved a fine balance with the help of a folded newspaper. For the three and a half day journey, I kept company with the

The 'hostiles', the Jarawa and the Sentinelese of the Andamans are the only tribes likely to survive, and this because they are holding off the outside world at arrow-point.

old gazette reports we'd tracked down about the history of the Andamans, interrupted sometimes by Annamalai's excited calls to come and see a school of dolphins frolicking along the ship's stern or, twice, to see a group of whales on the horizon.

The story of the colonization of the Andaman Islands by the British administration in India is one of high drama and tragedy, ending in1942 with the Japanese occupation, during which thousands of informers were tortured and killed by the invading army. For perhaps eight thousand years, the only inhabitants of these Islands were four groups of racially distinct tribes; the Andamanese on the Island of Great Andaman, the Onge of Little Andaman, the Jarawa, now confined to a reserve on the western coast of Middle and South Andaman and the Sentinelese on the Island of North Sentinel, just west of the Labyrinth Islands in South Andaman. They hunted the endemic wild pig with their bows and arrows or speared fish and sea turtles for food, occasionally driving off ships which tried to anchor on their territory with a stream of arrows. Their primitive lifestyle and negroid features brought them the hostility of merchants and other, sometimes nefarious, sea farers like the Malay black-birders or slave pirates who came into contact with them. Reports of the Island people became more and more exaggerated: "People on this coast eat human flesh quite raw, the complexion is black, the hair frizzled, their countenance and eyes frightful, their feet are very large, and almost a cubit in length....".

In 1789 Lieutenant Archibald Blair of the Indian Navy was entrusted with surveying the Islands in order to find safe harbours "where fleets in time of war can refit by any means... or to which any part or the whole army may retire in the event of a disastrous conflict with the Enemy...". Blair's report led to the colonization of Port Cornwallis, present day Port Blair. The settlement was later shifted to North Andaman but was abandoned due to the prevalence of cerebral malaria. During this time, contact between the tribals, the Jarawa and the Andamanese, and the settlers consisted of brief encounters, with bows and arrows pitted against British army weaponry. After the end of the unsuccessful venture the tribes were left in peace for a while; but then, some sixty five years later, in 1857, came the Mutiny and the need to accommodate the thousands of mutineers sentenced to life imprisonment. To this end the notorious penal settlement was established at Port Blair, and the effects of this move were disastrous for the Andamanese and Jarawa inhabiting the Island of South Andaman. These two groups reacted differently to the invaders of their land, and their future destiny was to be determined by the degree of their contact with the outsiders. The British began a process of taming the Andamanese with gifts and by the construction of a home for them to which friendly individuals were transferred. Very quickly, the new diseases to which the tribals had no immunity began to take a heavy toll and syphilis, measles and pneumonia killed off perhaps half their total population of four thousand eight hundred. None of the hundred and fifty infants born in the Andaman Home survived beyond two years. By 1931 their numbers had dwindled to ninety and the Superintendent of Census Operations, MCC Bonington noted that "this devastating fall in the numbers of the Andamanese in less than 75 years of contact with the administration paralyses comment". Today only twenty Andamanese survive and are heavy opium users, a habit they indulge in by trading bird's nests, ambergris and turtle shells with passing boats. The extermination of this five thousand strong tribe of hunter-gatherers must be laid squarely at the door of the British colonial government.

Fortunately for the Jarawa they kept aloof from the invaders except for occasional mischief — mainly in the form of raids on the settlement — for which they were punished out of all proportion to their crimes. A series of punitive missions against them left possibly hundreds dead. There is a record of one such conflict where the Jarawa killed four convicts from the penal settlement one year that triggered a retaliation in which thirty seven Jarawa were shot down. In his book, *The History of our Relations with the Andamanese* (published in 1899), Portman, one of the early administrators in the Islands, talks about the little known reason behind the friction between these tribals and the colonists. "On our arrival the Jarawa were quiet and inoffensive toward us, nor did they disturb us until we took to continually molesting them by inciting the coastal Andamanese against them. After a few years of this disturbance the life of the Jarawa became very hard and in retaliation they began to attack us". The handy policy of divide-and-rule was deliberately applied to the fragile Andaman situation as well, where the friendly Andamanese were given rewards for their help in persecuting the Jarawa.

The Onge of Little Andaman fared better than the Andamanese because their territory was not taken over by the government as was Great Andaman. But the brutal intrusion caught up with them and their numbers fell from about seven hundred in 1901 to two hundred and fifty in 1931; today there are a mere hundred and three survivors, mainly living in and around Dugong Creek, and government officials are pessimistic about the tribe's survival. It was the Sentinelese who proved in the end to be the shrewdest and thus the most successful survivors. They resisted all attempts by the administration to befriend them, almost seeming to divine the fatal consequences of a sudden contact with the

Attempts to contact the Sentinelese islanders have always been met with a shower of arrows. The Jarawa however, have started responding to the gift dropping efforts of the administration, the first step to their extinction.

outside world. It is still impossible to approach the Island of North Sentinel without attracting a hail of arrows from the Sentinelese, about whom nothing is known, not even their exact number; estimates vary from fifty to one hundred and fifty.

In an article in Britain's *Sunday Times* magazine of 14 September 1975, the photographer Raghubir Singh describes his dramatic but unfruitful attempt to make contact with the Sentinelese, along with an official government team and an Onge from Little Andaman who they hoped would act as a go-between. "Several armed Negritos emerged from the forest", writes Singh, "drawn bows in hand and arrows tucked in belts of bark. The Onge, holding a portable mike, shouted: 'We are friends, come close, we mean no harm'. The answer was the clang of an arrow against the side of our boat less than 80 yards from shore". Ultimately, in the history of the Andaman tribals, it may be this sound — the clang of an arrow — which is the sound of survival.

But back to our journey. On the fourth day, our ship the State of Haryana was gliding past tiny, glistening dots of Islands, always the same; a thick, green blob of jungle, with peripheral rings of mangrove forest and stark white beaches. By dusk we were in Port Blair harbour and the sequence of events there and over the next day in my diary are heavily decorated with pessimistic doodles. In the general flurry of activity at the docks our luggage was lost. It was finally located an hour later but by then the small band of Port Blair taxis had been engaged. Through the kindness of a local timber merchant we made our way to the rest house where we'd booked ourselves in to find there was no room. This was before the day of hotels, and we circled the town in despair for an age before getting an offer of a room at an ashram, a room stinking of urine and crawling with cockroaches; in the corners especially, the floor seemed to be alive with them. Later in the night, rats trotted boldly in and out, in complete charge.

A sleepless night later, the bad luck was holding out. In the morning we were waiting for a crocodile egg collection permit at the Forest Department office on Chatham Island when the clerk cannily began to question our bonafides. 'Name is Whitaker, no? Whitaker is foreigner, no? But you are Indian or foreign? — Please show passport, police identity'. My protest that I was not required to carry my passport around in my own country only aggravated the already shaky situation and the outcome was that we would have to get police verification of our identities in order to stay on in the Islands. 'Otherwise madam you will please to return to mainland with immediate effect. You are not possessing the necessary papers'.

They gave us instructions on how to get to the police station but it seemed unlikely that the police would be willing to verify the nationality of someone they hadn't set eyes on before. On the way there we passed the Wimco factory and Fate finally relented; I remembered the name Fred Burn, Wimco's manager, who was a ham radio friend of my uncle's. For years they had laboriously contacted each other on the wireless and through a deafening crackle, discussed the weather since all other subjects seemed to be taboo. So we took a chance, found Fred and told him our sorry tale. He phoned the police and I was legal once more. That afternoon he took us home to meet his wife Jean, who offered us their guest room which was of course accepted with alacrity. The Burns became good friends of ours. Fred's sudden death two years later was a shock to his many and wide ranging friends, and thousands of grieving mourners gathered at his grave to pay homage to this most generous and kind of men.

The Burns' bungalow was on the crest of a hill overlooking Port Blair harbour and how well I remember sitting out on the lawn with Jean, watching the dark sea alive with the moving lights of fishing boats. Rom had asked us to go to the Island of North Andaman, reputedly the best crocodile area, but there were two days before the ferry, Cholunga left on the twenty four hour run to Aerial Bay which we had planned to make our base for a few days. Meanwhile, we visited local areas like Chiciatapu where the edible nest of the swiftlets are to be found, in the process almost getting run over by one of the three taxis in town while chasing a green day gecko across the road.

One afternoon we got permission to visit the evocative ruins of Ross Island which used to be the headquarters of the British administration. The Chief Commissioner's palatial bungalow had fallen to pieces through disrepair; in the large ballroom a huge banyan tree had flung out branches which coiled around pillars and windows. In the officers' barracks we found many geckos and nesting swallows. Aplace of ghosts. Perhaps Lord Mayo had walked here in this very courtyard or corridor on the day he was murdered by a convict in 1871. And out in the bright sunshine, the graveyard overgrown with weeds, the loving messages covered with thick layers of moss. I rubbed and cleaned the epitaphs with a stick and tragedies sprang up around me like mushrooms; young officers killed by the Jarawa, children of three and four dying of disease. "Sacred to the memory of James Pratt, A.B. His Majesty's Naval Brigade, who was

Ghostly ruins of the cathedral on Ross Island, headquarters of the British administration in the Andamans.

killed by the natives of these islands on the 28th of January 1853 aged 25 years".

On the way to North Andaman the Cholunga stops at Strait Island where the handful of surviving Andamanese have been settled by the Government and given cows and pigs to raise. The boat picked up Loka, the headman, and his grand daughter. They were so youthful and lively that it seemed impossible to believe they were the last of their race. The sea was crystal clear and we watched fish, dolphins and green sea turtles swim below us as if under glass. At Aerial Bay we stacked our bags at the Forest Department's rest house and enquired about getting to the creeks once famous for saltwater crocodiles; Shantinagar, Shivpuri, Mugger Nullah among others. We were fortunate in finding a Bengali boy, Bimal Roy, who owned a dongy — canoe — and with him we rowed up and down the creeks adjoining the bay, often starting with the first glow of sunrise and returning at night with the oars throwing up flames of phosphorous. The schools of dolphins cavorting along the boat's side seemed to be playing with fire. Sometimes when the channels became too narrow or shallow we'd have to moor the dongy and continue on foot, a painful business because of the slippery mud studded with cruel mangrove roots. But we found little evidence of the once common salty except for the massive tracks of two wary giants who'd slipped into the water at our approach.

Talking to people in tea shops — a most productive censusing procedure — in the nearby town of Diglipur, we traced the predictable pattern of the crocodile's decline over the last ten or fifteen years. Poaching has been a fairly organised industry with two or three full time hunters who sent consignments of skins to the mainland regularly and used nets, hooks and traps with deadly efficiency. One of these, K, proudly boasted of his achievement in killing eight hundred and eighty three crocodiles and indeed his exploits made very interesting teatime conversation. He showed us one of his trophies, a metre long skull and gave me, with great reluctance, one of the teeth which looked more like a pig tusk. His prize catch was an almost seven metre giant and it had taken a hook, spear and several shots to kill the beast during which process K fell into its mouth, which it fortunately didn't close. It needed a crane to lift the crocodile into a truck for the ride back to Diglipur.

Apart from the hunting for skins, the fat, gall bladder and other croc parts that are used for medicine, the other factor responsible for the salty's sad plight here is that fresh water is a requisite and the females therefore have to nest at the top of the creeks with perennial fresh water. But these are also coveted agricultural and settlement sites and are thus becoming more and more populated. The collection of crocodile eggs during the nesting season, May to June, was the second most serious threat to the saltwater crocodile. At the time we were there, one could buy them for fifty to seventy five paise each. A year later Rom found several empty nests with the skeleton of the hapless female draped over it on Middle Andaman. Since saltys often come back to nest in the same spot and are so conspicuous both because of the large mound nest and their own size, they are perfect targets for poachers.

When not out on the creeks, Annamalai and I went into the forests behind the rest house looking for snakes and lizards of which we found several interesting species. Every log and branch in the forest is crawling with ticks, and in the tangled undergrowth it is impossible to avoid touching the dry branches and twigs on which thousands of parasites lie waiting for a juicy meal. We still remind each other of the bulging grey bodies which attached themselves to our arms, legs, backs, ears, between the toes and there were the clever ones which remained, tiny and undected, for days. But ticks apart, I began to understand Rom's fixation about this area. Not only is it incredibly beautiful, but the sunken mountain-top Islands contain unique fauna and flora much of it still unknown, representative of the Indo-Malay region. There are many endemic plants, birds and animals. These include twenty species of reptiles, such as the Andaman day gecko and the Andaman pit viper.

From Aerial Bay, Annamalai, Menon and I went down south — again on the Cholunga — to Mayabunder on Middle Andaman, the nucleus settlement of the Burmese Karens who were brought to the Islands by the British to work the timber. Although the Karen community is a well educated one, with men and women holding jobs in local schools and government offices, hunting and fishing is still a first love with many. They are the main suppliers of *trochus* and *turbo* shells which abound in the shallow coastal waters and which are used by the mother-of-pearl industry to make buttons and jewellery. These and other resources such as sea cucumbers and of course the abundant fish, could be considered for exploitation as an industry to protect the Islands from the ravages of industrial development. The coral reefs of the Andamans and the Nicobars may still be one of the most ecologically undisturbed marine systems in the world. During a later trip made together, Rom and I explored some of the reefs around Port Blair with the help of our good friend Dennis Beale and snorkelled through the wonder world of coral reefs, impossible to describe with justice. Resting briefly on the hard skeletons of the coral polyps we swam up to every shape, size and colour of fish, mollusc, marine worm, echinoderm . After dark, tiny luminous

The view from the Aerial Bay rest house on North Andaman.

organisms glowed through the silhouettes of coral gardens as we waded into the warm water for a nocturnal swim.

During our stay in Mayabunder we were fortunate in meeting and staying with a Karen family called Vaughan. One of the sons, Allen, who was later to become the first manager of the Crocodile Bank, took me to their family farm at Panighat, a short bus ride from Mayabunder. There we spent two days looking around the tick-infested forests for reptiles. He'd have his pack of hunting dogs with him, crashing excitedly through the forest, whimpering and yapping as they caught the scent of a wild boar, monitor or spotted deer. Allen crashed along like a boar himself, slashing wildly but always accurately at branches to cut us a path, with me breathlessly following. Again, ticks descended on us with radar like precision; in the evenings the clean floors of the Vaughan house were splattered with second hand blood.

Much of what Allen and I were exploring was not primary forest but secondary growth, witness to the continuing and damaging forestry operations in the Islands. Right in the early settlements days, 'Elephant Bill' Williams who worked for the Bombay Burma Trading Company was sent to the Andamans to assess whether timber extraction on a large scale would be commercially feasible. He found that it would be more trouble than it was worth and recommended that the forests be left alone. Later, well known foresters of the Indian Forest Service, like HG Champion as well as ecologists expressed their hope that the forest would be left intact.

But unprofitable forestry is apparently somehow desirable and massive amounts of timber have been extracted. Official reports on forestry in the Andamans make it sound as though everything is hunky-dory and all that soil erosion and reef siltation just isn't happening. Unfortunately, the thin topsoil of these tropical forests is quickly lost once the tree cover is removed. The natural regeneration that is supposed to be rejuvenating the forests is unsuccessful in keeping up with the pace of timber removal.

One morning we found an Andaman cat snake, one of the eight or more species of endemic snakes in these Islands. I was chasing a day gecko on the roof of the Vaughan's farmhouse when there it was, its thin delicate neck almost under my foot. '*Andha saamp, andha saamp*' (blind snake), farm workers yelled and we were soon considered heroes for handling the deadly venomous snake that was even reputed to breathe fire! And here I must confess that Annamalai and I assumed it was a pit viper and carefully pinned the head in order to hold it up for a photograph.

A year after my first trip there Allen Vaughan was with Rom in the Andamans when they were lucky enough to find a saltwater crocodile nest. They had a permit to collect eggs for the Government's crocodile project on the mainland but so far every nest they'd found was either an old one or a fresh one with the eggs robbed. Allen had brought a few eggs from Diglipur market but they had been tossed around too much and the chances of any hatching were minimal. Then they heard that several female crocs had been killed on nests at a new settlement area called Kishorinagar near Kalighat. They got on the Cholunga to Mayabunder the next day and from there the speedy M-5 to Parangara, a small town on the edge of a dense mass of mangrove channels originally named Congo Bay. Once they had explained their presence at the local teashop, run by Bengalis and complete with *rasagollas,* they got offers of several enthusiastic guides.

The rest of that day and half the next was spent slogging through heavy strands of grass, pandanus, cane and bamboo along the freshwater streams just adjacent to the mangroves, perfect nesting places for crocodiles. It was a bit scary, considering our experiences with captive saltwater crocodiles, and Rom carried a stout stick, even though it was clumsy. They separated to cover one particularly dense area, all of them moving on hands and knees through the eerie tunnels of vegetation. Minutes later Rom almost bumped into the nest which was in a clearing obviously made by the female crocodile. He couldn't believe his luck and made a cooing jungle call to alert Allen and the guides. A quick answer told him they were on their way. The first thing he did was to look around carefully for the female. There was no waterhole or wallow that she could be lying in and the nearest channel of water was fifteen metres away. He looked around for a quick escape route in case she suddenly charged from the water but it was tight vegetation all around except for the tunnel he had crawled into.

Allen came crawling through. followed by their friends from Parangara. 'Hah', they said in unison, happy that they'd finally found a nest. 'Where's the female?' asked Allen. 'Did you chase it away?'. 'No, I looked for it and it doesn't seem to be here'. They all peered doubtfully into the dark vegetation around them, the sun was almost totally blotted out and it was steamy hot, like in a greenhouse. They scraped the leaves and sticks off the top of the huge nest (nearly a metre high and a meter and a half in diameter) and yelled with excitement on seeing the gleaming white eggs. Everyone posed for a photograph crouching proudly beside the open nest. Just then Rom, now accustomed to the heavy shadows, perceived the outline of what looked to be the open, heavily toothed jaw of a crocodile under a thick pandanus nearby. He hissed a warning and as he pointed everyone backed away, peering under the bush. 'Yes, its the female', said Allen, 'and we'd better be sure she doesn't attack while we're taking the eggs'. They tried to head her back towards the nearby channel but she held her ground, hissing ferociously but restraining herself from charging. When they saw that she wasn't going to move they felt confident enough to extract and pack the fifty one eggs, using humus and leaves from the nest to cushion them, and began the long walk back to Kalighat. Rom came back to Madras soon after and a month later thirty seven hatchlings emerged, probably the first saltwater crocodile eggs to be collected and hatched under captive conditions in India.

In Mayabunder, Jerry Vaughan's house on stilts was on a rise with the ocean below on three sides; a view fit for a king. On my first trip, Annamalai and I had set out one night with him in a dongy, from his own private jetty, to fish for mackerel. We were heading towards a small offshore island across a quarter mile stretch of sea when the oar snapped and Allen crashed down at our feet from the triangular helm of the boat. In the confusion the better part of the oar fell overboard and was gone, which quickly ended the general atmosphere of gaiety. '*Ayyo sami*', muttered Annamalai, tightly clutching the sides of the violently rocking boat. But Jerry managed to look confident and in control, pounding the water with the foot long oar stub while the boat raced in the wrong direction with the wind. 'We'll wait awhile', he said when the wind died down somewhat — as if the decision were his — and we all threw in our fishing lines and caught, between us,over five kilograms of prime fish. In an hour it was fortunately very still and we started home, mostly a metre forward and a metre back. But we made it finally, and were able at last to scramble on to the sharp rocks towards the small, brightly lit house across the reef.

The shallow, reef ridden waters just off the west coast of Middle Andaman are the hunting grounds of both the Karens and Jarawa and encounters are increasingly frequent, as both groups have to go further and further afield to find good hunting and fishing areas. Exactly a year after my first trip there, a group of Karens were out diving for *kloe-suchhi* (trochus shells) and after a tiring day camped for the night on a small uninhabited island, Mowar Tikri. Unfortunately for them this was within the confines of the Jarawa reserve, off limits to outsiders, and as they made their evening fire a group of Jarawa planned their attack. At dawn there was a loud zing!–an arrow went through a diver's chest and everyone rushed towards the dongy anchored just offshore. The Jarawa charged, and kidnapped one of the party; he has not been heard of since.

The Trunk Road of South Andaman. Road work had to be abandoned after several road workers were shot by Jarawa arrows.

We met one of the luckier ones, a plucky twelve year old who dived between the forest of legs and escaped.

Just south of Aerial Bay is the stretch of bamboo where local farmers have seen several King cobra nests and from where Rom was to write in the June of '77; "Yesterday's walk was not exactly a normal excursion through the forest, it turned out to be more interesting than usual. One of the farmers had been cutting bamboo a month ago and saw what appeared to be a nest of some sort on the ground. It sounded very interesting so we made our way toward his farm by a path that cut along the pandanus lined beach, through the mangroves and across several large streams, the home of the salty in this area. A big water monitor startled us, charging across our path and as we walked we flushed out an amazing variety of birds, butterflies and lizards. It was the first sunny day that week and everything seemed to be taking advantage of it. We watched a pair of Andaman day geckos on their palm tree near the path and several day skinks, from the massive thirty five centimetre Tytler's to the high diving tree skink. The black-striped skink slithered through the grass to the safety of the thorny cane and palm tangle, and green forest lizards of many colour variations clung to nearly every tree in some areas. As we waded across one of the deep streams we saw a large, green tree snake and got a close look at this beautiful animal with its fantastic colours and excellent camouflage.

"The old farmer was waiting for us and we set off at a good pace to a small hillock below Karmatang Hill, the second highest hill in North Andaman. Crossing a stream we entered the uncut, unmolested rain forest and started uphill, among the abundant leeches which were only partially discouraged with the raw tobacco smeared on our legs. We finally got into the bamboo belt and saw the king cobra nest, 30 cm high and 60 cm wide....

"In the evening, over venison curry and rice in a wooden house in the forest, we listened to recent accounts of crocodile adventures and about Islands where you cannot sleep on the ground at night for the numbers of amphibious sea snakes coming ashore to lay their eggs"

West of Mayabunder, across the Austin Strait is the twenty kilometres long Interview Island where three years later Rom was to spend several days camping with photographer Rajesh Bedi, in an effort to publicise the urgent need for protecting these Island ecosystems. The ecology of Interview has been seriously affected by the introduction of elephants in the 1950s, by a Bengali timber contractor, PC Ray. He started an ambitious wood extraction operation there, complete with trolleys and tramways, the ruins of which are scattered through the jungle. The business went bankrupt, Ray died soon after and the labourers, tired of waiting for their pay, walked off, mahouts included, after freeing the elephants in the leafy Interview forests to wreak havoc. Rom and others found plenty of fresh signs and there are estimated to be thirty to fifty of these feral jumbos several of which are known killers, reputed to chase people on sight. A tricky problem for wildlife authorities!

The cultural and ecological drama being played out in the Andamans has become something of a crusade and Rom and I have travelled to our Islands of paradise many times, singly and together. One of these trips was not a particularly happy one; our friend Dennis Beale's boat dropped us at an Island off Port Blair where we wanted to camp for a few days and explore the coral reefs. On the second evening I took off my mask and snorkel in the shallows to find myself bleeding profusely; I was five month's pregnant at the time and there was no way of getting to a hospital. Fortunately, it did not develop into a great medical crisis but when we got back to Port Blair and were preparing to go down to the Nicobars, Rom began feeling ill and turned a bright yellow. The local doctor put it down to the sun. 'Please take your rest sir, you are simply exerting too much', but Dennis agreed it looked like jaundice. And to cap it all, I began to shiver violently on the way back to Madras: malaria. My parents took charge and off I went to hospital for ten days while Rom was fed vegetable soups at home.

Our appeals to Government to stop the tide of destructive development have been largely ignored; plans on the anvil include extensive plantations of exotic cash crops, more timber industries, even a duty free port in the Nicobars that we have opposed through a media campaign. The early response was that our reports were 'unduly pessimistic' and based on 'limited information', but concerted pressure from conservationists has had some effect and recent indications are that management trends may change for the better and at least a few of the Islands may be saved.

In 1984, Rom was asked to give a talk in Cambridge on the endangered environment of the Andamans. He produced a report which was widely circulated, and published by the department of environment in Delhi. In 1986, the Indian National Trust for Art and Cultural Heritage (INTACH) asked him to be its Convenor for the Andaman and Nicobar region. It seemed like a good platform to get ourselves heard from, and early the next year we set off, with flippers, snorkels and children, for our first visit in several years.

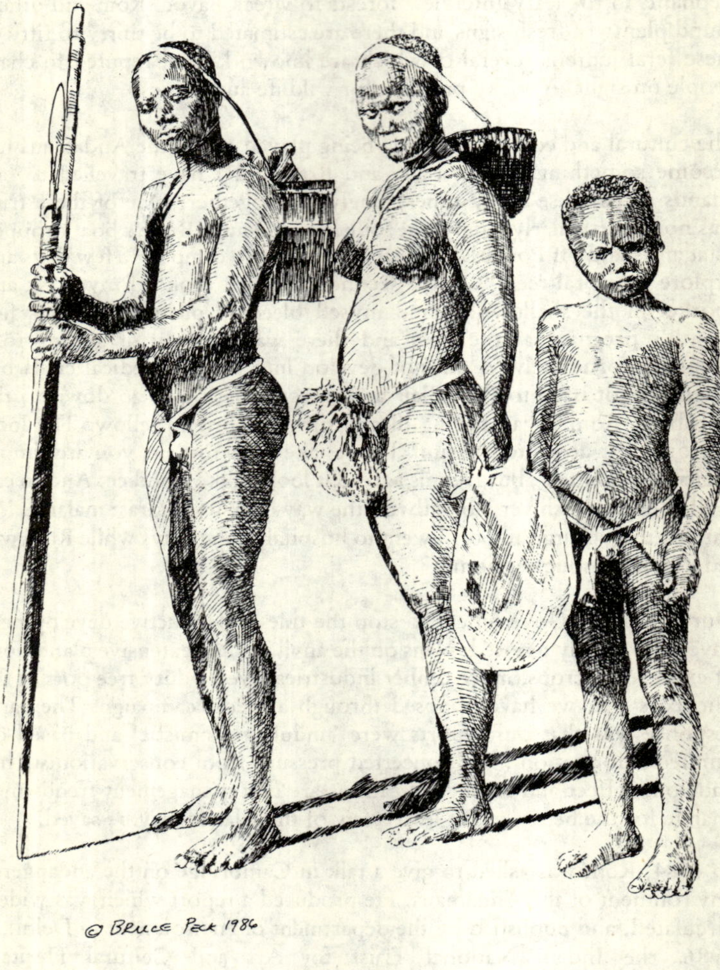

The Onge tribal reserve of Little Andaman is rapidly being deforested for settlers and oil palm plantations. There is little doubt that this will spell doom for this small, unique negrito tribe which today is reduced to under a hundred people.

Predictably, the Islands were noticeably changed and Port Blair's already unplanned appearance was converted into the chaotic bustle of any mainland town complete with traffic jams and garbage. Although lip service had been paid to the moratorium on the cutting of virgin forest and to forest regeneration, it was evident that the demand for these tropical timbers on the mainland is unrelenting. The blanks in the forest remain weed choked with little indication of the original forest coming back.

The tribal situation also continues to be grim: the Onge of Little Andaman and the Shompen of Great Nicobar are encouraged to barter their nutritious jungle foods like honey, for the poisons of civilization, tea, tobacco, polished rice. The Onge, who formerly had seven hundred square kilometres of tribal reserve land have now been herded together on a one hundred and ten square kilometre area known as Dugong Creek, complete with wooden and tin sheds for 'civilzed living'. Their demoralization is almost complete, and only a reversal in policy which could convince them that we respect their way of living — instead of their being overawed with ours — would possibly save them.

During the fifteen day visit we witnessed the army blasting coral reefs and primitive rock formations for practice, heard strange tales of absurd development plans going awry, met people who advocated taming the indigenous tribes. Underwater, we looked at acres of dead coral at boat jetties. It was apparent that the best thing we could do via INTACH was to organize an environmental awareness campaign with children as the target audience. We met and talked to a lot of people, notably some very aware and enlightened members of the Rotary Club and a few young scientists from CARI (Central Agricultural Research Institute) who made us feel a lot more optimistic about achieving the campaign.

Our 'big brother' in the Andamans is Captain Dennis Beale, a human gem who is known and liked all over the territory and who probably knows the Islands and their waters better than anyone else. He was one of the post war adventurers who helped to open up this area, with the Forest Department once totally dependent on his log hauling boats. In more recent years he has provided tourists in the Andamans the means to visit the charming little Islands in the Labyrinth group off the southwest coast.

One of our dreams is to join forces with Dennis in Port Blair, and make the Islands our home, once the children are grown up and choices involve only ourselves.

the crocodile bank

The very low and steadily decreasing numbers of crocodiles in India, resulting from the dual problems of poaching and the rapid disappearance of their habitat, predicted a grim future for these toothy reptiles, survivors of gigantic ecological upheavals for a hundred million years. The high price of their skins and the low pay of the enforcement officials made adequate protection difficult and under the cirucumstances the only likely answer seemed to be a captive breeding programme which would establish a safe 'gene pool' of breeders. In 1974, soon after our marriage, we decided to try and establish such a crocodile bank. From this, surplus offspring could be offered to Government for release in national parks, reserves and other protected habitats. This raise and release approach is very suitable for crocodiles, since most of the world's twenty two species breed well in capacity. Crocodiles are easy to capture and transport, and captive reptiles do not have problems adapting to the wild as mammals do.

At first we tried to find a sponsor for such a bank and the fat files of back and forth correspondence are witness to our failure to do so. But wedding gift cheques from my parents, grandparents Kamoo and Hassan Ali, and uncle Salim Ali could be used to buy land, and the Snake Park trustees agreed to meet a part of the initial expense of constructing enclosures and fencing. The Madras-Mahabalipuram road with its high, perennial water table, pleasant scenery and captive tourist flow was an ideal location and we spent many days driving up and down trying to pin-point the two acres we needed with the desired requirements. These were: a suitable price for our light pockets (land on this coastal belt was then four to five thousand rupees an acre), easy access from the road, and the willingness of the local village population to live with crocodiles. Finally, our choice settled on Vadanemmeli, thirty five kilometres south of Madras; there were two acres for sale, running, ideally, from the road to the sea shore and thickly planted with casuarina, the local cash crop which is harvested every three or four years. We clinched the deal, for which Rom had to consume several half litre tins of toddy with the owners. Immediately after, we formed a trust that later bought over most of the land leaving us half an acre on the beach. We have lived here since 1976. Pieces of adjacent land were acquired as money became available and today we own an acre and the bank over seven and a half acres.

After that things moved quickly. As at the Snake Park friends stopped in to help and the construction of the first crocodile pit was supervised by Jimmy Yacob, a young Malaysian Tunku who now works for Zoo Negara in Kuala Lumpur. A nucleus group of thirty five mugger were shifted from the Snake Park to their new home and of these, eight females and a male were released into the large hundred and fifty metre circumference breeding enclosure, built with a grant from the New York Zoological Society and World Wildlife Fund. Both these organisations have played important roles in the development of the Croc Bank. We also collected funds for the Bank by other means. In '79 Rom organised another snake show along with Kartikeya Sarabhai of the Nehru Foundation for Development in Ahmedabad. About 75,000 people came to the five day exhibition and half the ticket sale proceeds went into our first croc enclosures.

The breeders had been collected from various zoos, colleges, aquariums and wild habitats with permission from the Forest Department. Two of the females had been captured from the Chidambaram Waterworks reservoir. Night after night of setting traps and nooses and waiting for a croc,to find that one had veered a couple of inches at the last minute. Once in pitch darkness on the banks of the reservoir we were rolled up in sleeping bags, ready with nets and ropes, when we heard a thrashing in the bushes where the trap had been set. We both woke with a start, grabbed the nets to throw on the trapped crocodile and sprinted to the spot five metres away. And there, in the dim moonlight, was a large paddy bird flapping madly in the bushes. At two in the morning, it wasn't funny.

As the mugger were introduced to their new Vadanemmeli home, the stud Perayur,(Tamil for old man) quickly took charge of the enclosure and swam powerfully up and down the twenty five metre long pond, tail arched out of the water in a territorial display. He patronised the females in a manner that was almost human, now and then extracting a brief show of respect from them in the form of a raised head or rub on the jaw. For the next eight years he proved an excellent breeder, diligently courting and mating with five — and later seven — females and producing in all over one thousand five hundred babies. In the summer of 1983, Perayur dug a deep tunnel in a sand bank to escape the summer heat and suffocated to death when it collapsed on him. And to all of us at the Croc Bank it was like the passing away of an old friend.

Perayur, called Beta in some of ou- papers, gave us our first glimpse into the fascinating world of crocodile behaviour. This at a time when few behavioural studies had been carried out on crocodilians per se except those of Hugh Cott, Tony Pooley and Alistair Grahame on the Nile crocodile in Africa, and Jeff Lang on the American alligator. The Indian species in any case were a blank page except for the fact that the Jaipur Zoo had bred them, and some naturalists, such as KS Dharmakumarsinhji and JC Daniel, had made observations during the course of other studies. I became especially interested in the habits of the mugger. Before the children were born, Nikhil in '78 and Samir in '82, and my time was, incredibly, my own, I spent many hours in a hide in Pit 8 during the nesting season. On one such occasion I had been watching Perayur court Alpha, the oldest female of the group, with three attending females sort of keeping guard. One of these disappeared and ten minutes later a croc head appeared over the wall of the hide! From then I never entered Pit 8 without a stick. The information thus collected later formed the basis of several papers and articles.

The inter relationships among the muggers in Pit 8 turned out to be far more complex than we had imagined. During the mating season, which begins in south India with the north-east monsoon in November, we watched with surprise the gentleness with which these modern day dinosaurs played out their courtship dramas. In the typical mating sequence, a male approaches a female, who raises her head in a gesture of submission, and the pair rub the undersides of their jaws together and circle each other in a solemn, slow merry-go-round. Sometimes the male submerges and blows bubbles. Actual mating takes place several minutes after courtship begins.

Rules for hand feeding crocs: keep your finger nails short and your eyes on those jaws.

Mugger have proved to be runaway breeders at the Crocodile Bank and total almost three thousand at the time of writing. Fortunately, crocodiles are surprisingly restrained eaters; their metabolism is slow and energy conversion rate high, another factor which makes them ideally suited for captive farming. An average adult crocodile, say two and a half metres long and weighing seventy kilos, eats only about three kilos of meat a week. Luckily for us, they seem to be on a perpetual slimming diet. A light bulb hung in the hatchling ponds attracts varied and nutritious insect life and it is fun to watch the young after dark, agilely jumping up to catch fluttering moths and termites. After several weeks this diet is bolstered with *tilapia* fish which are common in the vast backwater that borders Vadanemmeli village. Mole crabs, the collection of which provides a little pocket money for our village *thambis,* are also fed to the crocs.

Adult mugger and salties get beef and large bandicoot rats that are brought by the flamboyant Kurvikaran or bird people, a hunting tribe conspicuous by their green berets and muzzle-loaders slung over the shoulder. The Kurvikaran are the only examples we know of tribal adaptation to urban living; they make themselves at home on the pavements of Madras city and proceed about their business with not the least paranoia and with a fine devil-may-care attitude. They eat practically anything that moves. jackals, every kind of bird including crows and vultures . We have seen them roasting whole pussy cats at their Adyar encampment, expertly turning the meat over a fire of cycle tyres!

The other two Indian crocodilians, the saltwater croc and the gharial are less adaptable captives than the mugger. Salties in particular create a housing problem because they will not get along amicably, and various serious injuries at the start made us realize that the policy of divide and rule would have to be applied. The Central Leather Research Institute in Madras was engaged, at the time the Croc Bank was getting underway, in studying the growth rates of five Malayan salties in the context of commercial farming for skins. They were planning to kill them in order to determine the size increase in captivity and were easily convinced by us that this could be done just as effectively by keeping them alive. The salties came to the Croc Bank on the agreement that regular growth data would be supplied to the Leather Institute. A pair of these is now breeding and producing over forty babies each year. The salty is the only Indian species of crocodile to build a mound nest; this is often a metre high dome of leaves, vegetation, and earth, and the eggs are laid in a conical depression near the top. After laying her eggs the female is like a dragon protecting its treasure, and short of breathing fire she plays the role faithfully. This makes the collection of the eggs for incubation a difficult exercise. At the nest site, in pit 2, two people with long poles have to keep her at bay while a third scrabbles nervously at the vegetation covering the eggs and transfers them to a box as quickly as possible.

Even after the eggs have been collected, the female defends her empty nest energetically. Our house is just east of the salty breeding pen and peering into it during evening strolls often produces an instant charge from her, as if on some electric cue. It worries me that one day one of our sons — both clandestine croc-pit wall climbers — might fall in, but Rom assures me that sensible crocodiles will reject them at once. The trouble is of course that crocs have so little sense.

The saltwater crocodile is the traditional maneater of the croc tribe because of its large size and fearless temperament. The largest at the Croc Bank is a massive, jowly individual called Jaws III who had to be consigned to solitary confinement last year because of his refusal to get on with others of his species; even females were greeted with a powerful attack. He weighs three hundred kilograms and the operation of transferring his residence was fraught with the sort of frightened hilarity well known to croc handlers. At one stage, while he was being released into his new enclosure, half the thirty or so people holding him panicked when he made a sudden lunge, leaving the others to their fate, which could have been disastrous. Everyone panicked and ran off, shoving and pushing in their eagerness to reach the small exit. Jaws III made the headlines the next day in the local newspapers and became one of the better known crocs at the Bank. The other such star was Heyward, the American alligator, who for a dozen years was the only alligator in India. He was a gift from Rom's friend Heyward Clamp, who keeps several in his backyard in South Carolina. Unfortunately, Heyward died last year and we never could discover what killed him.

Across the road from the salty enclosure are the gharial, who for the tourist, are the ideal introduction to crocodilians, being so unaggressive and easy to approach. Our son Nikhil often arrives at feeding time to help the keeper throw in bucketfuls of fish towards the long toothy jaws a metre away. Gharial feed exclusively on fish, though at the Croc Bank they eat mole crabs as well. So far only platonic relations and infertile eggs have prevailed among them and the difficulty in breeding them in captivity may confirm the thesis that they require deep, cool waters to breed in. This would be a pity because our gharial group includes four mature females and a male who has grown the prominent *ghara* (pot) on his nose, a sign of maturity and one which gives the species its name.

For our sons Nikhil and Samir, the Crocodile Bank is an ideal place to grow up with the sea, sand, wide open spaces, and plenty of kind and indulgent assistants who, unlike their parents, never say 'No'. Among the crocodiles, there is never a boring moment; they are either hatching, or being measured, or fed, or transferred to other enclosures. Both the boys are growing up assuming that having a couple of thousand crocodiles in one's backyard is quite normal. I recall Nikhil's first question to a boy in school, 'How many crocodiles does your Dad have?' and his surprise at the reaction. Nikhil, now seven, and his life among crocodiles was the theme of a film that became quite popular has been shown several times by the national television network, Doordarshan. As a 'star', he is often waylaid by groups of tourists, usually schoolgirls who pinch his cheeks and get a mighty scowl in return.

Our younger son Samir, just over the Terrible Twos (and into the Terrible Threes), is more of a snake man. He practically lives at the Irula Cooperative venom centre and most waking hours are spent stalking, pinning, bagging and releasing belts, strings, pipes and other objects that may pass for a snake. More recently, the process of venom extraction has taken up his time. A rope-belt is carefully pinned to the ground, held behind its neck and the venom extracted into a cup. During the release operation which follows, the belt is often let go with such force that it lands on his head, a frustrating experience for a young snake handler. In the evenings after his nap, Samir becomes 'Chockalingam', the Irula snake catcher who is his dearest friend, and woe be if one forgets and calls him by his own name.

But Samir's snake catching skills extend beyond ropes and strings. Recently, while Rom and I were away in town and the children were at home with the servants, a bronze-back tree snake zipped into the house. Snatching up the children, the two maids zipped outside screaming. The snake made itself comfortable behind the speaker in the sitting room. Finally, the long impasse was broken when Samir, on his insistence, was carried in and let loose in the sitting room. He waddled out with the snake in a few minutes and let it go off into the bushes. Samir and Nikhil know they can catch harmless snakes like bronze-backs but it has also been drummed into their heads that venomous snakes are to be left alone.

The tropical climate of south India is well suited to rearing crocodilians and the 1978 meeting of the Crocodile Specialist Group of the IUCN, the International Union for Conservation of Nature, held at the Crocodile

Bank, agreed that the Bank should become a breeding centre for all species, an ambitious scheme which may never be fully realized. But a beginning has been made in this direction, with a group of spectacled caiman from Heyward Clamp, Siamese crocodiles from the New York Zoological Society, African dwarf crocodiles from Zoo Negara and offers of other species. New pits have to be built every year as the population escalates sharply with over one thousand hatchlings last season. Over half a million tourists visit the Bank annually and the income from ticket sales supports maintenance, keeps the crocs on rats and fish and allows some development. From the beginning, the local labour force of Vadanemmeli village has been utilized exclusively, so that the Croc Bank's prosperity reflects directly on the village exterior and the lives of the villagers; the input of cash from salaries and daily wages has resulted in better housing, health care and education. Many villagers not directly working for the Crocodile Bank make a living by exploiting the tourists who stop at the village, selling coconuts, cane hats, snacks, cold drinks and coffee for a good profit.

The greater space and lesser number of visitors at the Croc Bank makes it easier to deal with the 'people problem' than it was at the Snake Park. But even so, difficulties often arise, especially on holidays when bus loads of brew happy tourists think that the ticket is a licence to behave as badly as possible. Most of the ugliest incidents follow a typical pattern; tourists breaking off branches (from carefully tended trees), attacking the crocodiles with this and other ammunition, trying to jump into the enclosures, and assaulting the assistants when asked to stop.

Individual tourists can also behave strangely. One morning I was sitting in the office overlooking Pit 8 (the mugger breeding enclosure) when two legs slithered down the wall on the other side; mysterious, since cleaning time was long over and anyway, none of the staff wear bright red and white checked trousers while raking away croc faeces. I hurried over and there was an American tourist taking a leak, with horror dawning in his eyes; for three metres away was Nova clambering up the bank. 'Hey! There's gator in here!' he yelled, frantically trying to scramble over the wall. He explained that he'd thought it was a toilet! Then there was the Frenchman who got very irate when stopped from leaning down and waving his hand in a rearing enclosure. He even hit the assistant who was trying to save his life. A big crowd collected around Monsieur whose few words of English proved inadequate for an explanation. 'I want only, only, I want only,' he repeated louder and louder. Fortunately, his wife managed to take him away.

One of the initial goals of the Croc Bank — to restock wild areas — has been rendered superfluous in a sense because at the same time that the Crocodile Bank was established, the Government of India with the help of the Food and Agriculture Organisation set up its own network of breeding and rearing centres that we initially helped stock and which are now producing offspring on a large scale.

These too are in a quandary since they exceed the numbers which can be released, not usually because of the lack of suitable habitat but because several state governments believe that crocodiles are detrimental to fishery operations and therefore are reluctant to 'spoil' their commercial fisheries industries. So far four hundred and sixty mugger have been given by the Croc Bank to the Forest Departments of several states for the purpose of restocking wild areas. But there is a glut of mugger on the market due to the good work of people like Binod Choudhury, Lala Singh, D Basu and Sudhakar Kar of the National Crocodile Project.

What is in store for these thousands of surplus mugger in the several breeding centres all over the country? It is time to at least start thinking about the implications of commercial crocodile farming in India for the skin market which would value a three year old mugger, whose total food expenses would be about five hundred rupees, at two thousand five hundred rupees: a sum the average labourer in Madras would earn in four months. This single dynamic fact stands up and holds its own against the often woolly philosophies of the 'total preservationists' who are shocked at the vulgar suggestion that animals should be killed for commercial gain. But a continually empty stomach can bring about a fine change of views.

Many naturalists in India agree with the rationale behind skin farming but argue, quite reasonably, that once the market is recreated, it will be a bottomless pit into which both legally farmed as well as wild poached skins would fall. In Papua New Guinea the legally harvested skins were tagged with a government tag and were then registered with the export authorities. Our two years of involvement with the skin industry there showed us how very suitable the crocodile was as a 'crop' in developing countries, with its low maintenance needs and high gain. The skin trade in Papua New Guinea earns an income of two million dollars every year, much of which goes directly to subsistence level tribal communities living in inland swamps where any kind of agriculture is impossible.

Apart from supplying mugger for release in wild habitats, the Croc Bank's major contribution has been as a public education centre. Through signboards, guides and of course the exhibits themselves, the tourist who thinks he is just walking around is actually picking up interesting information which would broaden his attitudes to the natural world. He is able to identify individual crocodiles by their plastic tail tags, learn their names and buy a feeding ticket which allows him to have one of the assistants feed the animals for him to see, and even throw in some fish himself. As at the Snake Park, we often hear about people for whom this direct contact with the crocodiles and their problems in the wild creates a new and zestful interest in all wildlife.

The Crocodile Bank is in touch with many 'crocodile people' in other parts of the world, some of whom have visited Vadanemmeli as part of their own research. In 1978 the working meeting of the Crocodile Specialist Group of the IUCN was held here and the exchange of ideas on site with crocodile savants from other countries was useful and stimulating. Fred Medem who was at the helm of crocodile conservation in South America was there, as were Wayne King, the group's Chairman, Ted Joanen, and others. One could never sit down to a meal without a mention of sexing techniques, unformed embryos, gall baldders, and so on which I, in my third or fourth month of pregnancy, found a little hard to stomach.

Along with the effort to change people's attitudes about crocodiles and their necessary role in the environment goes a parallel programme of research on the behaviour and biology of the Indian species. Results of behavioural research, which adds to the sum total of our knowledge about wildlife, is in itself worthwhile, but sometimes it goes beyond that and contributes to influencing the ultimate fate of the animal. Studies at the Croc Bank have revealed two incredible facets of the mugger which will revolutionize farming techniques.

The first is that the mugger at the Croc Bank do not follow the egg laying pattern of other species of crocodiles. All crocodiles are supposed to lay one clutch of eggs each season, but the 'mug' has not read the books, and lays two. This is such a diversion from normality that at first we could not explain the extra nest in Pit 8. The next year there were two 'spares' and so on until today, when seven females lay eleven nests altogether (three lay a single clutch; four are 'double clutchers'). There was considerable discussion about this at the meeting of the Society for the Study of Amphibians and Reptiles on crocodile biology at Milwaukee, Wisconsin in 1980, at which Rom gave a paper on the mugger. The reason for this aberrant behaviour was conjectured to be the high summer temperature and food abundance at the Croc Bank. So far this is the only place in the world to record the double clutching behaviour.

The second discovery is even more interesting and has perhaps a deeper ecological and economic significance. Scientists have found that the sexes of some freshwater turtles are not determined genetically, but actually in the egg, by the temperature of the nest. The same has been found to be true for the American alligator and some marine turtles. This discovery may finally swing the balance in the controversy about whether characteristics are genetically inherited or moulded by the environment. Scientists may prove once and for all that the environment is the stronger and more powerful factor of the two.

In 1983, the American crocodile biologist Dr Jeff Lang, from the University of North Dakota, began a study at the Crocodile Bank on the mugger's breeding biology and specifically on the issues of sex determination and the mystery of the double clutches. We'd first met Jeff in Port Moresby, Papua New Guinea where he was studying the New Guinea freshwater crocodile and salty. Later in 1980, we stayed with him and his anthropologist wife Gretchen, before the Milwaukee crocodile conference and Rom put himself in Jeff's capable hands regarding the presentation of our paper on the biology of the mugger. Writing it had been easy but to make it interesting and stimulating to a scientific audience was another matter. With this, as with numerous other projects, Jeff's help was invaluable.

Observations are made at night when mugger females usually nest, so Jeff works at night and sleeps during part of the day; for him lunch time is midnight, and the best time to see him is 2 am. So far his data confirms that sexes of mugger are determined by the incubating temperature and in a very cut and dried way. Females are produced at all viable temperatures but males predominate at high temperatures. So you can have controlled situations with fairly simple equipment to 'run off' males, females, or a proportion of the two. This opportunity of monitoring and arranging sex ratios is of great importance to the big commercial croc farms in the United States, Africa and elsewhere.

As is the case in India with practically every group of animals, so little is known about the natural history of crocodiles here that something new turns up all the time. This year one of the nests in Pit 8 was not detected early enough, and hatched naturally in the enclosure. The mother crocodile scrapes the earth away from the nest hole when the hatchlings beep from inside the eggs, and carries the hatchlings and partly hatched eggs gently in her jaws to the water. We were watching this in June when

'Holy cow!', said Jeff. It was not a female this time but Makara, the male who'd taken Perayur's place as the stud for the group. The large lumbering male was performing all the maternal duties himself! One of the hatchlings had fallen into a depression near the nest and he nudged it into his mouth and slithered down to the water. This was the first time that a male mugger was found to participate in nest excavation. In South Africa, the naturalist Tony Pooley has photographed a Nile crocodile male roll unhatched eggs in his mouth in order to help release hatchlings from the egg shell.

In 1981, the Crocodile Bank started a freshwater turtle research and breeding programme. By that time Vijaya Jaganathan, one of the Snake Park volunteers, had completed the first freshwater turtle surveys with World Wildlife Fund sponsorship, and had a collection of almost half of the twenty six Indian species, several of which were breeding in captivity under her supervision and care. It soon became obvious that freshwater turtles were another unknown group of reptiles. Turtles are eaten by tribal people all over the country but there is one state, West Bengal, where hundreds and thousands of turtles are brought in from all over north India for their meat. In 1983, Dr Ed Moll of the University of Illinois, spent nine months in India gathering data on the distribution and status of turtles. He made the Bank his base camp, living between endless train journeys, in a leaky, rat infested hut in the Croc Bank compound which he maintained was 'just great', and which Jeff Lang later inherited. Both became expert rat trappers.

Satish Bhaskar — the sea turtle man — and Vijaya worked with Ed on the turtle surveys and they put together reports on the status of freshwater turtles in India. Methods used were river netting, interviews with fishermen and turtle catchers, and visits to markets where turtles are sold for meat and as a cure for tuberculosis. In West Bengal and Uttar Pradesh particularly, thousands of freshwater turtles are slaughtered every year. Although West Bengal is the main market for turtle meat, they are caught in all the states bordering the Ganga and transported hundreds of kilometres by train to Calcutta. Turtles share the peculiar fate of snakes in India; they are both worshipped as well as killed by the thousands. Turtles are considered to be another form of Vishnu among the Hindu pantheon, and many Hindu temples, such as the one we visited in Tripura, have a population of sacred turtles which are regularly fed by visitors. In Bangladesh, the unique black soft shell has survived only because of the religious protection it receives at the Biazid Gostami Shrine outside Chittagong, where pilgrims feed them puffed rice, bananas and bread on bamboo skewers.

Turtle man Ed Moll arrived at the Crocodile Bank at a time when Nikhil, five, was full of insatiable curiosity about reptiles. During the months that he helped Ed, Nikhil learnt a lot about turtles.

Ed Moll worked mainly in Uttar Pradesh, Bihar, Madhya Pradesh, Andhra, Orissa and West Bengal and when he left India, Vijaya began a study under him on the rare cane turtle of the Western Ghats. She had rediscovered this species after about seventy years during which time only two captive specimens had been identified. She worked on its natural history and that of its eco-counterpart, the Travancore tortoise. During the cane turtle study Vijaya lived in a large cave at Nadukani Reserve Forest in Kerala, which Dr Brian Groombridge, of the Species Monitoring Centre in Cambridge, England, has pronounced to be one of the healthiest surviving rain forests in south India.

In June '84, our secretary Brenda Bhaskar and I set off to visit Vijaya in her cave and arrived at the town of Chalakudy early one morning after a sleepless train journey. But the forest officials were not too keen on allowing us into Nadukani. 'How do we know you will not take away specimens?' I explained that we only wanted to visit Vijaya and that in any case there was so much poaching going on from every account that taking away a few specimens would not matter; it may even save them from being killed. Of course, our popularity plummeted further but we did get a permit for Nadukani. An autorickshaw took us to Kodali from where we hired a Jeep to take us to Anaipandam, a small camp where a group of Kadar tribals have been relocated by the government.

Halfway up the two hour climb to the camp it began to rain, drenching us and our knapsacks which felt like dead bodies. Luckily, we'd met Chandran, a Kadar tribal working for Vijaya, or we might never have found our way in the wet darkness of that evening. 'How much more?' we asked him again. 'Just a little', he answered pointing beyond the sunset. I had just come out of hospital some weeks before this after an appendicitis operation. The steep trek up and later the bounding from rock to slippery rock on grassy hilltops made me wonder if I'd flown the coop too soon. Brenda generously shared my anxiety. 'Walk slowly, or you'll open up again'.

We arrived in inky darkness and soaking wet at Vijaya's cave home, fifty metres above a stream frequently used by elephants, and kept a wary look out for them later while bathing in the chilly water. The rocks were smeared with yellow powder which turned out to be homemade bark soap which Chandran's family used. Later on we watched his wife, Laila roast and crush snail shells to fill her lime container. Over a dinner of rice piled with fresh mushrooms Vijaya summarized the progress of her study in the tracts of evergreen forest at about six hundred metres. Here the cane turtle leads a most un-turtle like existence, scurrying under leaves like a lizard when startled and feeding on fruit, mushrooms and insects. We turned in early to bed, which was a section of the steep cave floor, down which we slid by degrees during the night. At midnight there were cries of '*Yaanai, yaanai*', (elephants), and Brenda and I shot up ready to run. But it was only Chandran's aunt having nightmares.

We spent the next day with the Kadars, looking for turtles in the forty two hundred metre grids which constituted Vijaya's study area. Just before leaving camp we were putting on our damp, steaming shoes when a scorpion careered up Vijaya's leg. It was quickly apprehended with a twig and deposited on the camp's periphery. Down in the valley there was soon that familiar cold sensation between the toes and we stopped to pick off leeches with a dab of salt; though we soon gave up to avoid being stationary targets. By midday Chandran had a cane turtle and a Travancore tortoise; the latter seemed to favour open rocky places and later we found one wedge sideways between two boulders, and rescued it.

At dusk a large flock of Malabar hornbills flew noisily overhead and we looked up at a fruiting banyan tree laden with parakeets, scarlet minivets, nuthatches, grey hornbills, orioles and sundry other birds I was unable to identify. At times like this I wish — but only briefly — that I had availed of the numerous attempts made by my father and uncle Salim to knock the names of some of the commoner birds into our heads when we were children.

The only snake we saw that day was a hump-nosed pit viper, which is apparently very common in Nadukani. Several of the larger trees supported the dizzy bamboo ladders that the Kadars use during the honey collecting season. Using the flexible parallel support, they lever themselves skyward after dark, often to thirty metres and more to collect the honey from large hives of hill bees in order to sell it to a local cooperative. There was elephant dung everywhere, and a few weeks after our trip Brian Groombridge was lucky enough to see a troop of lion tailed macaques, the rare endemics of south-western India. But already the signs of doom and destruction are evident in Nadukani; it is obviously on the hit list of the timber merchants.

There was no transport for us the next day so we took a leisurely six hours tramping back to Kodali, the nearest bus stop. Our batteries were recharged every couple of hours when we came to a stream or river and, throwing off our knapsacks, dived in for a soak.

After half a century of no reports, Rom and Mohammed Ali Reza Khan of Dacca University found that the batagur turtle is alive and doing fairly well in the Sunderbans, in both Bangladesh and West Bengal.

Another exciting discovery was the finding of *Batagur baska* alive, but not so well in the Sunderbans. This is the largest Indian hard shelled turtle and there are reports from the turn of the century about the harvest of millions of these turtles and their eggs on rivers like the Hoogly. But the turtle had been unreported in this region for the last sixty or seventy years. Then in 1981, when Rom was at Dhaka Zoo with Reza Khan, a friend of ours at Dhaka University, they saw a large *Batagur* with its distinctive turned up nose which the keeper said came from the Sunderbans. A year later Rom was surveying crocs in the Bangladesh Sunderbans and met fishermen who routinely catch the turtle they call *kata*. They kept several alive in small ponds near their houses for eventual sale at the market. They caught them on hooks baited with mangrove fruits. Soon after, during our surveys on the Indian side of the Sunderbans, Vijaya found them being caught and kept in the same way.

A generous grant from the Wildlife Preservation Trust International enabled us to begin a systematic study of captive freshwater turtles, by building a large deep pond in which eighteen Indian species are kept. The most impressive inhabitants of the pond are the huge soft shell turtles, some of them thirty five kilogrammes in weight. One of these behemoths is a Leith's soft shell which was gifted to Ed at a temple tank in the hinterland of Andhra Pradesh. This extraordinary gift is a good advertisement for Ed's pleasant nature and winning smile. During September this year two Ganges soft shells dug nests and laid twenty four eggs each. This is a happy event in itself, but more important, it tells us that the size and design of the pond do cater to the needs of the turtles. Aside from just wanting to find out about the turtle's breeding habits, we had other important reasons for starting this breeding programme. The soft shell turtles are true river vultures and help keep our rivers clean. Half burnt corpses would litter our northern rivers if it wasn't for the turtles. We found that hard shelled turtles can devour huge quantities of water weeds, like hyacinth, and hope to prove that turtles can be effective answers to weed choked waterways. The Government of India's Ganga cleaning project has now included a turtle rearing component, much to our satisfaction. And one of the most important reasons for perfecting turtle husbandry is to demonstrate that Bengalis could be living on home grown turtles instead of continuing the destruction of the wild populations.

In March '87 we had a short but lucrative visit from American turtle man Mike Ewert. He opened our eyes to a lot of amazing facts about turtle breeding and got us on the way to solving some of our most perplexing

Munnuswamy of the Crocodile Bank holds a chitra. This is a soft-shell turtle which was described by a turn-of-the-century naturalist as growing big enough to upturn a small boat. Chitra turtles can grow to a metre and a half in length.

turtle questions. For example, how did our flap shell turtle eggs develop almost full term embryos, then sit and wait for six months before hatching? Once they hatched to the stimulus of a hard rain beating on the roof of the lab in which they were incubating. Mike explained that the embryos know that the time to pop out of the egg is when there is adequate rain to form the ponds and streams they need to live in. If they hatched into the hostile hot season they probably wouldn't survive twenty four hours.

Another question was why our north Indian turtle eggs, obviously fertile in the beginning, only developed for a couple of months then gradually died. Mike deduced from examining this year's batch of Ganges soft shell eggs that the embryos had entered into a state called 'diapause'. This sort of suspended animation could only be broken or stimulated by the normal winter drop in temperature they would experience in their northern home. The way he suggested we solve this problem was by making a modified refrigerator to keep the eggs at fifteen to twenty degrees Celsius for forty to sixty days. At the time of writing, sixty Ganges soft shell eggs are undergoing this fridge treatment under the watchful eye of Chandini Menon, a voluntary worker.

Turtles in murky pools are not easy creatures to observe. But they soon learn to come at feeding time. In the new breeding pool they are gradually becoming more trusting and will soon be hand fed.

Tree ferns, which were here before the dinosaurs, epitomize the spectacular plant life that draws us back to the forest again and again.

a snake catcher's cooperative

At the time Harry Miller first introduced Rom to the Irula snake catchers in the late 60s, and later through the early development of the Snake Park, these tribals were the backbone of the snake skin industry in south India. Many made a living by selling snake skins to tanneries; twelve rupees per cobra, the same for rat snakes and Russells vipers, and less for smaller snakes such as checkered keelbacks and sand boas. Pythons had been over hunted and were becoming hard to find. A good day's catch could bring in thirty or forty rupees, plus very often the incidental benefit of some rodents or mongooses for the pot. A decent living, even though the rapid spread of suburban Madras meant that they had to go further and further afield to find productive hunting areas. Since the early 60s the Irula have also been catching common kraits, abundant in the scrub forest around Madras, for the Haffkine Institute's antivenom production unit in Bombay.

With the setting up of the Snake Park, Rom came face to face with the colossal strength of the snake skin market for the first time. He and other conservationists like my father and JC Daniel, realized that the industry would have to be closed down or closely regulated in spite of the jeopardization of the Irula's interests. And in fact, they were echoing the fears of herpetologist Malcolm Smith who wrote about over exploitation of snakes back in the 30s in his *Fauna of British India* series. The skin trade's ecological implications were already apparent in the massive grain destruction by rodents once their main, most efficient predators — snakes — were removed from fields and adjoining forests. Though we have only preliminary data on the percentage of rodents in the diet of free ranging snakes, there is plenty of qualitative evidence from agriculturists to show that removing large rat-eating snakes from an area is a direct invitation to the ravages of rats. One estimate is that these pests destroy a staggering thirty to fifty percent of the country's stored and standing grain every year. The director of a group of tea estates in the Nilgiri Hills visited us to ask if the Snake Park could supply him with rat snakes to release in his five thousand acre plantation, since the natural predators of rats such as snakes and birds of prey had disappeared following the removal of adjoining forest tracts. His estimated annual loss was five lakh rupees. Apart from destroying the roots of tea plants, the prolific rat holes weakened slopes, causing erosion and landslides. A rice farmer from Cumbum Valley, in Madurai district, wrote to say that he followed the increasingly common practice of hiring Irula rat catchers every season, paying a bounty of one rupee per rat. He claimed this worked out far cheaper than the damage they caused to his crops. On the governmental level a rat advisory board was constituted to evaluate and control rodent damage. At the same time, an average of five million snake skins were being exported each year; the Adam tannery in Madras did a brisk five thousand skins a day during the boom period between the early 50s and 70s.

In 1976, the Government of India banned the export of snake skins and put a stop to this wasteful trade. But for the Irula hunter gatherers the new legislation was disastrous; they lost their single effective means of earning a livelihood. The psychological implications were as important as the practical. 'I've always thought of myself as a snake catcher, and been proud of it', said Natesan to Rom. 'Now I must be like everyone else, grubbing around in the city for work, like a bear digging for termites'.

The skin trade ban was actually the last of a chain of events over the years which had increasingly frustrated the Irula tribals, about sixty thousand of whom live in the plains of Tamil Nadu in Chinglepet and neighbouring districts. The scrub forests which had been their hunting grounds disappeared under the heavy wand of development. Places where they had hunted monitor lizards, mongooses and other game became the city's margins. Further, most species that were important food requirements, except rats, were included in the Wildlife Protection Act of 1972, a very timely and necessary piece of legislation but which disregards the whole question of local protein sources. It is oblivious to the fact that local populations get their protein by hunting small game. In time, the most common species of soft shell turtle, the food of thousands of protein starved tribals and rural Indians, was protected under the Wildlife Act, and the penalty for catching, buying or using these prolific turtles is up to six years in jail and a heavy fine.

This dual role — that of befriending and working with the Irula and at the same time campaigning for the closure of a trade so vital to them — was an uncomfortable one for Rom; he was working both for and against the Irula's interests, a paradox about which Natesan needled him often. 'Hey man, you give us money with one hand, and take it away with the other!' In actual fact, he and many others realized the scientific necessity for terminating the skin industry with a far sightedness which in retrospect seems quite remarkable.

A group of Irula including Natesan came to Rom one day and asked for help in applying for farm land to the Government. But they soon agreed that it would not be a workable proposition; their instincts and traditions are based on mobility and the solution lay elsewhere. Rom began to work on a proposal which would use their snake catching skills within the framework of the new laws.

Slowly, things started coming together. If the Big Four venomous snakes were caught by members of an Irula cooperative, and released back into the wild after several venom extractions, it could become a viable and worthwhile project. Not only would it resurrect the Irula's occupation and preserve their heritage as hunter gatherers, it would also play a significant role in the medical world. Antivenom serum is made by injecting snake venom into horses in increasing doses, then drawing their blood and purifying the serum which contains the vital antibodies that combat the invasion of venom. The production and distribution of antivenom serum was far short of the actual needs of the country and most health centres still do not stock it. An estimated ten thousand people die of snakebite every year, mainly because the antivenom is not freely available. A venom cooperative run by the Irula could save lives by supplying venoms of the Big Four, from which polyvalent antivenom is made. At the same time, the snakes would not be killed, making it a model wildlife management programme. An Irula venom industry, thought Rom, slapping Natesan on his back.

A draft of its detailed working structure was ready just before Natesan died. Unfortunately, he did not see the fruits of his long sessions with

Rom in the palm leaf office of the Snake Park. 'Do it, man, do it', he'd said,' it will be a sure good thing.' But the World Wildlife Fund did not think so at the time. Those were the'total preservation'days, a necessary stage to be sure in the evolution of wildlife conservation. Rom wrote to World Wildlife Fund which he still represented in south India and which has been his support from the beginning. Their response was a theoretical approval but a reluctance to be involved with a resource exploitation project. It is very much to their credit that ten years later the Indian chapter of World Wildlife Fund gave the cooperative a substantial loan which enabled it to shift its premises and get off the ground.

But to back track a little, in his reply to World Wildlife Fund International in November '73, Rom stepped right into the quagmire of the delicate issue of wildlife utilization. "I believe", he wrote "we have brought up a very important policy issue that cannot be quickly dismissed by saying that we (WWF) should not lend our name to schemes of controlled wildlife exploitation. In a sense we have already done that by endorsing institutions like zoos and the Madras Snake Park.

"The exploiters of wildlife are in a fairly secure position as long as they have only to deal with confused and vague local wildlife laws and petty officials. Perhaps it is time that the zoo trade, biological supply trade and the skin trade be gradually pressured into following the recommendations and rulings of the internationally prestigious World Wildlife Fund and the International Union for Conservation of Nature. The best way to know what is going on in this business is to be in it. Who is better suited to evolve and guide a scheme which, while carefully exploiting wildlife, also has a finger on the pulse of the trade than the World Wildlife Fund.

"If we help establish a biological supply house owned and operated by an Irula Tribal Co-operative and endorsed by our organisation we would soon know which animal species are in demand, where and how they are caught, transported and sold and in what numbers. Just this one positive aspect from support of a controlled wildlife exploitation scheme might prevent several animal species from reaching endangered status.

"The poachers and dealers in rare animal products are always a few steps ahead of us, because of the commercial motivation. The present WWF policy shows a weakness in an organisation dedicated to keeping animal species from extinction. At the frightening rate that wild habitat is being destroyed in this country there is no doubt in any of us that little wildlife can exist outside of sanctuaries. It is a difficult issue, I realise, but I believe that the organization and guidance of wildlife-economy based tribals is one step toward controlling the trade in Indian wildlife".

My father, then the Vice President of WWF-India and one of the Vice Presidents of the IUCN, was enthusiastic about this scheme and wrote to WWF-International that, "the sustained exploitation of all natural and wildlife resources is the basic policy of the World Wildlife Fund, and I think that Whitaker has raised an important matter and we should give it serious thought. I support his suggestion that an Irula cooperative be set up". My father also wrote to several government officials about Rom's projected scheme for the cooperative and there seemed to be considerable enthusiasm. Dr NR Krishnan, Director, Department of Science and Technology wrote, "I met Dr BD Sharma, Joint Secretary, Tribal Welfare and his assistants in the Ministry of Home Affairs on the 30th June 1977. I handed over to them copies of Romulus' paper. They evinced keen interest in the proposal and felt quite enthused about it...."

Venom is one of the most expensive natural resources on earth, five to a thousand times more expensive than gold, depending on the species. We like the idea that the Irula, one of the poorest groups of rural Indians, should produce one of the most expensive products in the country. A gram of krait venom costs three thousand rupees, ten times the current price of gold. About fifty kraits are needed to make one gram. In real terms that means fifty kraits are potentially worth three thousand rupees. In the skin trade, this quantity of snakes was worth not more than a few hundred. Thus, the venom industry would use far fewer snakes to generate much greater income for the Irula.

My father stressed repeatedly that the cooperative should be pursued and established in spite of seemingly endless red tape. He wisely realised that it would have important repercussions in the development of India's conservation policies. So, soon after in '78 we went ahead and registered it with the Industries and Commerce Department. The Forest Department was approached for permission to catch five thousand snakes per year for venom production, a number that one large tannery could have processed in one day during the skin trade. The project hibernated. As in the early Snake Park days when he was applying for land at Guindy, Rom laid seige at Fort St George, Tamil Nadu's administrative headquarters, knocking on the doors of tribal welfare and forestry officials and being told 'please come again next week'. During one such visit a fat cockroach scampered out in surprise when the relevant file was opened and we gave up for a while.

On our return from Papua New Guinea in 1981 we had the good fortune to meet and become friends with Revati Mukerjee, who was to play a key role in the cooperative's establishment. She had given up her job and was looking for something interesting and rewarding to do. We made her the offer of running a problem-ridden cooperative without pay. 'But in two years', Rom assured her, 'the cooperative will be rolling in the stuff, the Irula driving around in Cadillacs and you can name your price'. The reality was a little different.

After several months of energetic chasing around government offices Revati obtained the necessary permits and licenses and the cooperative was in business. Each of the initial sixty Irula members had an identity card and a license number. Detailed records had to be kept and submitted to the Forest Department, on the numbers and species of snakes caught and the amount of venom extracted. This was because all snakes are protected under the Wildlife Act. One of the conditions on the government order allowing us to function was that twenty five percent of the gross profit from venom sales would be paid as royalty to the Forest Department. This is surprising, to say the least, considering the cooperative is a tribal self help project and not a commercial business.

The first venom order came from King Institute, Madras, one of the five major producers of antivenom serum in India. The initial bugbear was now familiar to Rom; how to start operating as quickly as possible with very limited capital? All of us had pooled in our private resources to pay the fifty rupee membership for each Irula member besides which there were two thousand rupees in the bank from donations. This was not nearly enough to buy all the equipment we needed. The major expenditure was cages for the snakes and several carpenters were called in to give estimates, all of which were too high for our meagre budget. Finally, it was the simple clay pot which saved the day. Rom borrowed an idea from the snake catchers of Shirala where they keep their snakes in mud pots for the Nag Panchmi festival. At two or three rupees each they were cheap, cool, secure and easy to move around, the perfect snake cages. Wetted down periodically during the hot months and with a water dish in each, snakes thrive in them and mortality has been less than two percent.

Right from the start, functioning from a small room at the Snake Park on borrowed money, the cooperative has filled an important gap as supplier of high quality venoms and today its outstanding orders total over a kilogramme. Several individual donors and companies gave us help without which it would not have been possible to function. Our friends

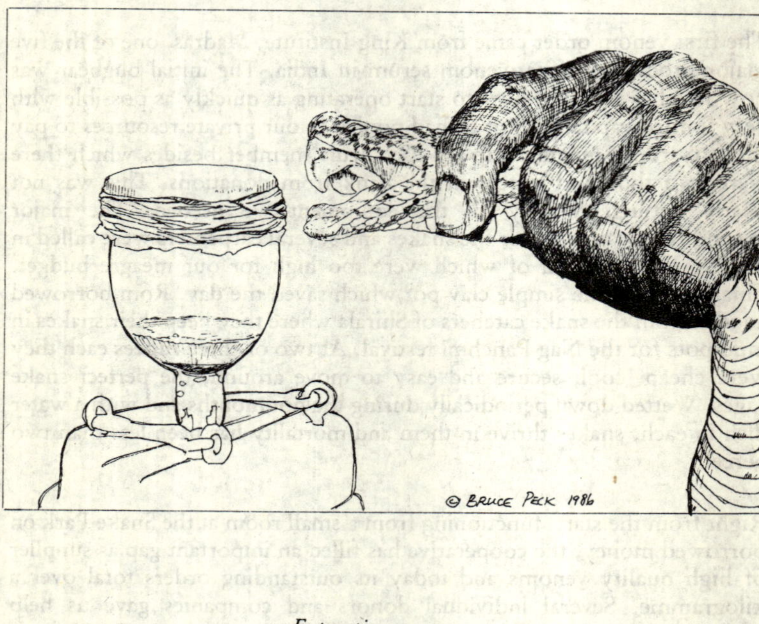

Extracting venom.

Dino and Sandya Mazumdar lent generous support and the British High Commissioner in Delhi gave us a sophisticated electronic weighing machine that was a vast improvement on the little jeweller's scale that swung wildly with every breath of breeze.

After a year of operating at the Snake Park, the Trustees of the Crocodile Bank very kindly agreed to give the co-op half an acre of land on a nominal lease. There was a lot more space here and tourists could come and see the snakes for a small fee of fifty paise. The gate collection now almost covers day to day expenses. On most days the licensed catchers start arriving by bus around 7.30 am with muddy snake bags. They come from Thiruporur, Perungalathur, Chitlapakkam and other Irula settlements. After a cup of tea and a chat, the process of buying snakes begins and Rajendran, the assistant to the manager and himself an Irula, weighs, measures, and inspects each snake. He marks it with a permanent code number by clipping a combination of its belly scales so that every snake that goes through the co-op is identifiable. Details of where it was caught and any unusual circumstances are noted down in a ledger and the snake placed in a vacant clay pot with its code number and species marked on the outside. K 468 for instance would be the 468th krait caught. In fact, K 468 is well remembered because it bit and killed Gopal, one of our best snake catchers.

What sets the cooperative apart from other venom production centres all over the world, is that snakes are only kept in captivity for three weeks. After three extractions of venom over this period they are released back into the wild. In other labs they are kept and extracted until they die. 'Release days' are busy ones at the cooperative. Rajendran puts up a 'closed to visitors' sign at the gates and he and Dorai start packing the snakes to be released. Often there are well over a hundred to be bagged. On one such memorable day in 1984, at the end of the saw-scaled viper season (the winter months), we joined the Irula in setting four thousand of these vipers free. It was quite a sight. It's amazing how hundreds of snakes can just disappear in the surrounding jungle in seconds. Nevertheless, you keep on your toes on the walk back to the Jeep.

So far a few snakes have been recaught and the cooperative has collected the first data on growth rates and migration of wild snakes in India. The co-op keeps careful notes about all the snakes and is scratching the surface of the mysteries of snake's lives. Rom made sure that such research becomes an important part of the co-op's operation. As he says, we must learn about the animals we use. Looking closely at snake faeces isn't everybody's idea of fun. But the co-op has been checking literally thousands of samples in the last few years, and has plenty of evidence to show that all these snakes prey largely on rats and mice.

Almost every day Rajendran and Chockalingam, members of the co-op who live on the premises and take care of the routine work, extract venom which visitors can watch. With expert ease, Chockalingam opens one of the clay pots and, with a snake hook, gently lifts a cobra onto the small central platform in the square pit where the snakes are kept. It is a smooth operation with a minimum of trauma for the snake which Choky makes graceful. The head is pinned to the ground with the rubber handle of the hook as he steps on the tail to give himself the proper leverage and to keep the snake from thrashing and injuring itself. He holds it carefully behind the neck so that it is unable to turn around and bite. This is a crucial stage, when most accidents happen; Russells vipers, for instance, with their long, curved fangs, can bite right through their lower jaw and into the thumb holding it. But Chockalingam is probably one of the best snake handlers in the world and keeps every contingency in mind as he plays this dangerous game with hundreds of deadly venomous snakes every week.

Thus caught, right hand behind the neck, left supporting the tail, the snake is carried to the conical venom glass clamped to a stand and with a piece of rubberized cloth stretched tight across the opening. One watches carefully at this stage and visitors hold their breath and comments as the snake's head is brought towards the venom glass. With a sudden forward jab the jaws clamp into the rubber sheet. Golden drops of venom, deadly but also life giving, trickle down the sides of the glass as the audience gasps, and begins to talk again; the tension is over. The quantity of venom varies greatly from snake to snake; one cobra may refuse to yield any venom at all during repeated sessions, while the next will bite energetically and spew a quarter of a gram. The saw-scaled viper's small size and vibrant energy makes it perhaps the hardest species to handle; besides, it takes roughly four hundred of these snakes to make up a gram of venom. One marathon day Chockalingam extracted six hundred of them and was bitten twice with little effect.

The liquid venom is frozen and dried under high vacuum. The powder retains its potency and antigenic properties. Bottled in powder form, it is easy to handle and send in the post. The Irula cooperative is now the largest producer of snake venom in India and antivenom production is dependent on it.

Rom's experience of working with Bill Haast at the Miami Serpentarium has been of great help in assisting the Irula to produce high quality venoms. Haast himself has been very supportive of the cooperative and its work. Producing venom involves much more than grabbing a snake and making it bite a container. Venom is a complicated chemical and high quality venom depends on the health of the snake, its food and care. Venom which is contaminated or not properly processed or stored cannot be used to make antivenom serum. Haast fed his King cobras a high protein mixture with a feeding gun, but at the cooperative the short duration of the snake's captivity eliminates feeding altogether. They are given water. Kraits, which dehydrate quickly, are fed a solution of glucose in the summer months with a modified syringe. Initially, Haffkine Institute adhered to its policy of producing its own venoms, but recently it started buying Irula products.

For the past two years the cooperative has been engaged with another activity; RATS, a rat and termite eradication programme. Rats are undeniably the scourge of man's crops and pesticides are no solution, apart from creating deadly complications. The Irula approach is based on their knowledge of the rat's natural history: they dig and smoke them out more efficiently than any poison could work. The Oxfam Trust in India supports this program and provides a Jeep which is used for the project as well as for the weekly snake releases. The idea germinated years ago soon after our marriage, when Rom and I spent a few days at the Central Food Technology Research Institute in Mysore with a group of Irula. The staff of the Institute were impressed with the possibilities of using the Irula as an alternative to pesticides.

So far RATS has concentrated on field trials. We must establish that it is economically possible to eradicate rats by using the Irula. In one nine month period in 1986, fifty six rat catching field trials were made where two thousand one hundred and thirty one rodents were caught. The cost of catching each rat was one rupee and sixty five paise. In this study, calculating the average amount rats eat and destroy, about fifteen thousand kilogrammes of food grains were saved, valued at forty five thousand rupees. The investment in Irula labour was three and a half thousand rupees.

The most destructive rat in rice fields in our area is the lesser mole rat while the bandicoot, house rat and the brown rat operate mostly in godowns and warehouses. These, plus a couple more, destroy a major percentage of India's food resources every year. The true potential of the rat's destructive powers really becomes apparent when walking with the Irula in the paddy fields. They often find five or six kilogrammes of rice, paddy or peanuts in just one rat hole; enough to feed a family for two or three days. Rom thinks that RATS has the potential to employ thousands of Irula and even other rat catching tribals.

The most obvious benefit of the cooperative for its members is of course the income from catching the Big Four snakes, and the welfare budget which includes money for school fees, uniforms, loans for house repairs and medical expenses. But much more important in the long run, the Irula have been drawn into a process of decision making and planned action which will prove vitally important in their future. Their new found self-assertion and confidence is more and more apparent at the general body meetings, which were initially silent affairs, at which our suggestions were met with acquiescent nods. It is no longer so. While discussing controversial issues such as snake prices and bonuses, three or four simultaneous arguments erupt and issues have to be voted on. But it goes beyond the capacity to decide; the Irula are learning the art of taking decisions that are unfavourable to them personally, but beneficial to the collective body of members. For example, last year a few members wanted the price of kraits to be raised. This was possible, but it would trigger a chain reaction which would be disadvantageous to the development of the venom market; it would mean fewer snakes, less venom, and the slowing down of business orders. It was finally decided to keep the same prices.

Again, last month a petition was received from three former trouble makers who had complained to the Forest Department about the 'mismanagement' of the cooperative. The group now claimed that they had been coerced into signing these allegations and resigning from the cooperative; but their wild accusations had contributed to the closure of the cooperative, for six months, by the government. The Irula had finally gone to court and obtained a stay order. Anyway, the little renegade group asked to be forgiven and allowed to become members once more. There was a long, heated discussion and both Revati and Rom encouraged the members to forgive and forget and take them back, pointing out that it was a victory for the cooperative that they wanted to return. But Rajammal, an expert snake catcher and one of the seven Directors of the cooperative, raised her fist and sat up on her haunches in readiness for a fight. 'Okay, *dorai!*' she addressed Rom, 'if we do as you say and take them back, and if they get up to the same tricks — then who will be responsible? You?'

On the whole, there has been a tremendous response to the cooperative's work, both in India and abroad. There has been support from many individuals and organisations, including Norad, Oxfam and WWF. But it

Ramachandran, an Irula Cooperative director, readies his hunting implements. He specializes in cobras and Russells vipers, the main snakes found near his village of Thiruporur.

has been through some bad patches, mostly because of allegations made against Rom which unfortunately were taken very seriously by the authorities. Although many local Forest Department officials have become good friends of the co-op, the paper machinery is often against us, because permits, such as snake catching licenses, take four or five months to renew. During this interim period, when they are not allowed to catch snakes, the Irula have little or no income. Recently the cobra and the Russells viper have been more strictly protected under the Wildlife Act and we have set in motion the lengthy procedure to apply for permission to catch these snakes. In all this paper work, it is not only the Irula who suffer, but the antivenom serum industry, which is already unable to keep up with the demand.

Practically every week, the cooperative gets a message to send the Irula to catch a cobra or viper in a house or compound in Madras. We have to write back and decline, saying these snakes are now protected, and we could be liable to pay a heavy fine, and have our licenses revoked. The next message we get of course, is that the snake has been killed, thank you very much. We hope that the Government will agree to give us special powers with which we can help stop the killing of these protected animals.

Along with Revati we are just embarking on another exciting project with the Irula; this time, with the women. In November '86 while sorting the otherwise mundane daily mail — requests for reprints, information on snakes, bites — we came upon a winner; approval of a grant from the National Wasteland Development Board for thirty lakh rupees or three million, for an agro forestry project. We had asked the NWDB to help us with land and jobs for Irula families through a new society, the Irula Tribal Women's Welfare Society. Most Irula women do not catch snakes and we wanted to break the male domination!

Then began the period of locating all the wasteland in Chingleput district that we could find and taking tea with village officers, revenue inspectors, tahsildars. Fortunately, the Assistant Collector of this district, Dr Prasada Rao, has been very helpful and interested. Finding land with no squatters or other claimants proved to be difficult but finally seven hundred acres were identified, and the paper pushing has begun.

Briefly, the project hopes to plant a thousand acres of wasteland within three years, and settle as many landless Irula families as possible. They will look after the planting and nurse these forests-to-be. In some ways this is one of our most exciting efforts; a chance to grow a forest from scratch, and to nurture a private ecosystem.

The venom unit, rat catching programme and now the tree farm, will slowly teach the Irula to take pride in what they have to offer, and rebuild the independence which is a prerequisite for tribal people to survive. And perhaps, in time, the cooperative will become a prototype for hunter gatherers all over the country and the emphasis will shift from teaching tribals, to learning from them.

another beginning

In the summer of '84 Rom was in Kodaikanal with the children and I was writing my graduation exam in English literature when an extraordinary thing happened. Someone claimed, and complained to the Forest Department, that Rom was involved in an illegal trade of reptile specimens. This resulted in the filing of a patently false case against him in court. Mark Davidar, the Manager of the Park and Shekhar Dattatri were also charge-sheeted and a vicious investigation followed. One immediate outcome was that the Irula Snake Catcher's Cooperative was closed down by the Secretary, Forests and Fisheries, pending settlement of the case. In a fine display of mental toughness the Irula decided to go to court against the closure.

Simultaneously, the group of trustees opposing Rom at the Snake Park filed a civil suit in the High Court, questioning his competence to run it. A similar case was later made against me, as Honorary Secretary of the Crocodile Bank. All this was the result of a situation which had been building up at the Snake Park for several years. The snake park was not developing the way Rom had envisioned. It was turning into a bureaucracy and the enthusiastic field work and research that were its' hallmark were shoved aside.

The various court cases are into their third year. Things were made so unpleasant for us at the Park that we mentally and morally withdrew from its management, leaving the field clear for the rival groups to take over. But it was not easy to walk away from a fifteen year investment of time and energy. It was an extremely sordid story and a depressing period for us, of tensions coupled with amazing insights into bureaucratic bungling. Sympathetic officials have told us pieces of the behind-the-scene saga; how, for instance, Rom was almost arrested, and plain-clothesmen were to be planted all around the Snake Park to monitor his activities!

But it is a story I had rather not dwell on; such things are better forgotten or those little seeds of bitterness tend to drain all the energy and space in one's mind. For a while I went under. Rom managed to continue functioning as productively as always, though he began to look gaunt and tired, and to question his choice of taking Indian citizenship if this was the reward.

Our parents and others backed us with all the livid loyalty of an enraged family. Shama's husband rushed to Madras in the middle of his hectic schedule, to give constructive suggestions about developing our legal defences, and Murad's wife Irmela, now a second sister, came several times to lend a sympathetic shoulder. The articles in the media about the 'specimens case' brought heartening supportive mail from all over the country. "I read about your supposed criminal activities", said one letter, "and it is the old story. Once something gets too successful, then the vultures move in". A lady from Delhi whose children were frequent visitors to the Snake Park wrote, "You have given up your own country to live here and serve in the interests of wildlife conservation, and this is what you get. But you must not forget that there are many like me who sympathize, and who are ashamed of what has been allowed to happen".

So we left the carcass and moved on; we made a conscious decision to cut off the Snake Park from our minds and Rom made it taboo to mention it at all. On one of the last days that we were at the Park, collecting our personal files and books, the erratic coin telephone rang and it turned out to be Montres Rolex from Geneva, giving Rom the news that he was short listed for their Awards for Enterprise for his work with the Irula Cooperative. Their representative was on her way to Madras for a final evaluation of the project. Coincidentally, Satish Bhaskar, the sea turtle man, was also being considered for the award and they both received an honourable mention and inscribed gold watches. Satish's project was a six month sea turtle study on South Sentinel Island in the Andamans, adjacent to the territory of the Sentinelese tribals who still shoot arrows at outsiders. His wife, Brenda, was relieved when he didn't win the award money which would have enabled him to stop the arrows.

Shortly thereafter, Rom received news that he would be given the Order of the Golden Ark from Prince Bernhard of the Netherlands and this brought the happy reminder that the litigation and scandal which had sprouted around us, was not the end of the world and that the essential value of our work was not being questioned by one and all. And later that same year-'84-a tour organised by our friend Dr John Constable, a surgeon at the Massachusetts General Hospital and a keen naturalist, visited the Croc Bank and sent Rom twelve thousand dollars in appreciation of his work. This windfall could not have come at a more opportune period. When we left the Snake Park we lost our transport, which made it very difficult to function productively. With the Harvard group's money we bought a Mahindra diesel Jeep and this has enabled Rom to resume his fieldwork and his lectures at schools and colleges.

One of the members of the tour group was Dr Stephen Jay Gould, the evolutionary theorist, who has been drawn into the limelight because of his heretic challenge to some of the basic tenets of Darwin's theory of evolution. While living out a personal tragedy, including a painful fight against mesothelioma, the cancer caused by asbestos, he has been at war with traditional Darwinists, supporting his theories through a hectic series of lectures and papers. Rejecting the hard core assumptions about adaptation, natural selection and the survival of the fittest that we all grew up with, Gould is proposing that other factors-and even chance-may have a lot to do with the way in which species change. During his study on a species of land snail in the Bahamas, he found that there were several variations, all of which true Darwinists would explain as features of natural selection; thick shells on the coast to protect them from crab predation, mottled ones in the interior for camouflage. Gould questions this assumption and says that adaptation to the environment and a selective growth or change do not necessarily go hand in hand; snails grow in different ways only because they grow in those ways, and every feature is not successful in terms of survival. He gives the example of the human brain which among other things has taught us the fact of our personal mortality. From Steve Gould, fighting against cancer and dependent on narcotic pain killers, this is a poignant example indeed.

The Crocodile Bank continues to flourish, with visitation rising each year as Mahabalipuram becomes an increasingly popular tourist centre. After the debacle at the Snake Park we have both been able to devote a lot more time to the Bank and projects long buried in dusty files have been excavated. The present Manager, Harry Andrews, has been with us since '83. He has a long association with forests and wildlife and his presence has made a tremendous difference, both to the general morale of the Bank as well as to its facade and maintenance. He is both a curator as well as a supervisor and his activities range from laboratory and research work to overseeing accounts and apprehending tourists busily throwing stones at the crocodiles. His active participation in the work doubles the efficiency and willingness of the staff. Too often, institutions in India are managed by standing at a distance-preferably in the shade-maintaining a false status quo and yelling at everyone else. Recently Harry's petite wife, Romaine, a professional secretary, joined the Croc Bank as Office Manager and we are now computerized.

The office has expanded considerably. Funds from Jeff Lang's mugger project have enabled us to equip a very efficient laboratory cum office which is the home of boxes of croc eggs, filing cabinets, typewriters and other paraphernalia. There is also a photo dark room that Rajendran from the village has been trained to use, and this facility has made our own 'reptile PR' work much easier. With careful watering and tending, the trees at the Crocodile Bank, mostly casuarina and neem, have turned it into a green sanctuary between long stretches of barren, hot sand. We have raised a nursery of six thousand trees with seeds from Auroville, and in a few years visitors will start getting lost in dark stands of bamboo! Several of the local tourists stop here on the way to Mahabalipuram to relax in the shade over a short picnic.

People ask how I spend my time in the isolation of our beach front home at the Crocodile Bank and the answer is that it seems to spend itself without much help. Because of the distance from town, evenings out are few and far between and films, plays, concerts and other events go by while we sit on the beach telling ourselves we're not missing much. Once in a while, the feeling that life is passing us by propels us into town but by the end of the long drive we are tired and have had enough. Home beckons strongly, and by the time the interval comes around, we are quietly sneaking away from art and culture.

Several strong interests have had to be curbed, living as we do beyond the end of the world, but others have taken their place; some, like sewing, a little reluctantly and with uncertain results. I churn out garment after garment which would have been great if a little different, and Nikhil has stated that he would prefer a tailor to make his pyjamas in future. A brisk walk in the evening on the beach after office and household chores makes

Our sons, Nikhil and Samir share an iron age dolmen with the old Irula snake man, Doraiswamy. Coincidentally, many of the settlements of these Irula aboriginals are situated at these ancient burial sites.

for royal entertainment, with perhaps an afternoon swim thrown in for good measure. And sometimes I sit at my desk at night staring at the piles of MA texts and wondering if I should actually open one of them.

On most days Rom is at his desk at the crack of dawn and is hunched over his clip-board or making rounds at the Croc Bank until six in the evening, our dinner time. We both work partly at the office and partly at home. The latter is preferred; our desks face the ocean which allows us to keep tabs on fishing activities. Often when a net is being pulled in front of the house we leave our files and rush out to buy a few fish. But because the typing and filing has fallen to my lot since our secretary, Brenda's departure a year ago, a good five or six hours have to be spent in the office. One of the more interesting activities I have been supervising is BEEP, the Barefoot Environmental Education Programme. We send boys from the village to give talks and slide shows at rural schools on different environmental subjects such as tree planting, snakes and so on. So far it has been on a very small, informal level but the response from schools has been fantastic. We have applied for funds to expand and improve the programme.

Rom seems to have made a habit of forming small groups of active people who generate interest and concern about environmental problems. One of these is the Madras Mahabalipuram Conservation Council, which comprises of residents of this coastal stretch and is trying to stall the spread of industry to this zone and indiscriminate tapping of the natural aquifer for the city's needs. The scenic Mahabalipuram coast is an important green lung for the weary Madras city residents and we are hoping it will stay that way.

When my father visited us in Kodaikanal a few years ago, he donned a white cap and binoculars and strode among the *shola* forests of these beautiful hills. He was dismayed at the mammoth conversion of the natural forest to eucalyptus plantations and potato fields. This had taken a dramatic toll; hillsides were sliding down at every rain and there was an acute water shortage, as the water retaining forests were being decimated. He wrote a report on this crisis, comparing it to the already devastated Nilgiris and pleading for a changed approach by Government. He noted that the botanical gardens had managed to propagate four hundred different species of roses and yet had never cared to grow a single *shola* tree. His indignation made itself felt in representations to the Government of Tamil Nadu and articles in the press. He also suggested that a local group of concerned citizens get together and form a conservation council.

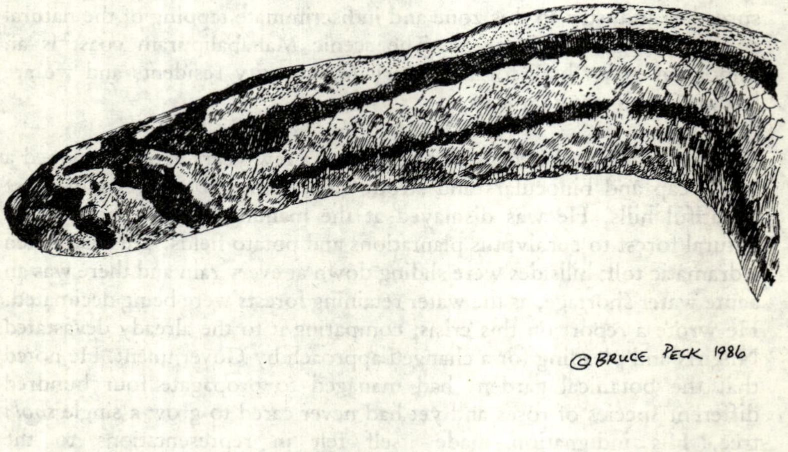

Both our boys have become good snake hunters. In 1982 Nikhil found this Kukri snake in Tiger Shola in the Palnis which turned out to be a new species, now named Oligodon nikhilii.

In the two years of its life, the Palni Hills Conservation Council has shown what a powerful force citizens can be. Thousands of *shola* seedlings are now being grown by the Forest Department, Public Works Department, and the Council itself. An afforestation plan for the new reservoir catchment has been formulated, approved and funded. On a larger scale, the National Wasteland Development Board has granted forty seven lakh rupees for planting trees in the Manjalar watershed, which is the reservoir one sees when driving up the Kodai ghat. This project was conceived and is being carried out by founding member C Jeyakaran (Jakes) and three tree experts from Auroville, David Nagel, Jean Pouyet and Navroz Mody. Like islands, hill stations attract a fascinating array of human types and Kodai is no exception. The PHCC consists of people like Jakes, who comes from one of the most influential families in these hills, and the Viraraghavans who grow prize roses and are dedicated ecologists. Another founding member is Father KM Mathew, a botanist who I can only describe and talk about in superlatives.

Our own one acre plot on the beach at the Croc Bank provides much scope for raising and tending plants, which we both enjoy doing. The bushy clumps of vegetation that have sprouted all over the garden have now been colonized by nine species of lizards, several snakes, a family of mongooses and many birds including partridges, kingfishers (white-breasted, common and pied), tree pies, babblers and many more. And last year we had a visitor who created quite a furore. Our dog Popsy began to bark hysterically at two o'clock one morning and Rom stepped off the back steps into the sand, forgetting his own unfailing advice to always carry a light at night. One pace later he felt something rough sliding away from under his bare foot, and at that instant a loud hissing filled the night and woke me from a deep sleep. Rom shot into the air, landing a foot away to see a large Russells viper coiled and ready to strike. He had been exceedingly lucky; he'd stepped squarely on the snake's mid-body, giving it time to snap back and bite. After securing it in a pillowcase we were too shaken to go back to sleep, so we sat up drinking tea and composed a song for the still hissing culprit:

Russells viper burning bright.
Do not hiss and do not bite,
We are trying to save your skin,
From handbags, wallets and their kin.

On getting married, at twenty, I stopped writing third rate poems, threw away masses of lines about heartaches, and turned to popular natural history writing. It is a profession I greatly enjoy. Freelance writing also allows for the time flexibility needed to run a family as well as a career. While we were in New Guinea, between '79 and '81, I held two or three temporary jobs and the uncivilized concept of having to be in office at a certain time every morning makes me appreciate this freedom all the more, and admire the mass of humanity which troops in and out of offices at predetermined hours. On the other hand, working within one's own time frame does of course have its limitations. There are days and days when one floats along unproductively, excusing oneself with all manner of conjured up reasons.

Having lost the Snake Park salary — about two thousand five hundred rupees between us — the small matter of income remains and in the last year we have turned to a new activity, which we hope will provide the economic stability required to continue functioning in our own sphere of interests. Together with Revati Mukherjee and Shekar Dattatri, we have formed a company called Eco Media which is making sixteen mm and video films on environmental themes. Our first production is a film about snakebite which was made in collaboration with our friends John and Louise Riber. John and Louise are Indian born Americans who, like Rom, studied at Kodaikanal School. They are film makers and have produced several documentaries on family planning, health, literacy and other third-world issues.

The film, called *Snakebite!* tells the basic facts about the subject; which snakes are dangerous, how to avoid getting bitten, how to treat snakebite should it occur. We now realize that the new medium of film is fantastic in its impact as well as its wide reach. The messages that were so painstakingly spread through the Snake Park and which reached a fraction of the people who most needed the information, can now, through television, reach millions just in one showing. Hopefully the impact of the film will not be merely to convince people of the medical necessity of using antivenom serum, but also to activate health officials into providing a better distribution of this life saving drug. Even as I write this, a snakebite victim from a neighbouring village who fortunately had a dry bite with no venom injected, went to no less than six primary health centres for treatment. None of these had antivenom, and one offered him a herbal preparation instead!

Filming *Snakebite!* was a wonderful experience in spite of the fact that things went wrong wherever possible and we were working on it at a time when our personal lives had taken a toss due to the Snake Park drama. The Serum Institute of India in Pune came through with a grant of fifty thousand rupees for the film but even so we were working on a rock bottom budget. Most of the location filming was done in the scrub hills around Madras, often at sunset since 'dusk shots' are John Riber's passion. 'Let's get the krait at sunset, you guys.... I can just see the orange glow reflecting on its blue-black scales....'. And so, sunset after sunset, we filmed cobras and kraits, Russells vipers and saw-scaled vipers-the Big Four-in an effort to help people identify and avoid them.

We had our moments. Several weeks of being in such close contact with venomous snakes naturally brings some excitement. While involved in close-up macro work, John would be too engrossed in manipulating his lens to protect himself adequately as well, and it was up to Rom and Shekar to keep the fine balance between technical finesse and safety. Sometimes the balance tilted slightly. We found that snakes are not naturally photogenic and getting a single shot right could mean days of trial and error.

During the opening sequence we needed a cobra to sit up, hood spread, then 'de-hood' and slowly crawl away along a bund. Easy as this may sound, it drove us all mad as every cobra wanted to do anything but that. We finally found one cobra which, during two dress reharsals, complied with professional ease. He stood up, expanded his ribs to spread a nice big hood and, a few seconds later, slid calmly away along the bund with the sunset gleaming on his back. We'd found our man. Ecstatically, John crouched into the mud and levelled the tripod in readiness to start filming. And just then Nature pulled a dirty one on us. From the open sky, a spotted owlet dived down like a rocket. It aligned its flight path towards the cobra and struck the snake on the head with its talons, displaying such force that our star collapsed and later died. My father suggested that the owlet was nesting nearby and therefore was defensively aggressive. But to our minds the little wretch was being just pure wicked.

On another occasion it was people who went out of control. The film begins with a sequence where a farmer is attacking and consequently being bitten by a cobra. He dies as a result of treating the bite with chants and herbs instead of antivenom serum. For the dying scene we got together a few of the Irula shamans to chant and sing *mantras*, while the actor, Sathy (who was supposed to be dead) looked furtively around as the scene became more and more emotional. Finally, two of the women became quite hysterical, urinating all over the floor and rolling back and forth as the dead man beat a hasty retreat.

Soon after *Snakebite!* was completed, Rom wrote a story for children about a little village boy who makes friends with a crocodile, and ultimately saves it from getting killed by the adults. I converted this into what we hoped was a screenplay and we sent it along to the Children's Film Society in Bombay which funds childrens' films. To Rom's delight and my horror, it was approved as a ninety minute feature film, in Tamil. We are now in the process of finalizing the contract with the CFS while rooting up cinematographers, translators, production assistants and the many other professionals we will need.

So here we are, at the crossroads again. It is difficult to tell what the future will bring. Our association with the Crocodile Bank, the Irula Snake Catcher's Cooperative and other projects remains as strong but the main parking lot once filled by the Snake Park is now empty. Perhaps films and writing will fill it, perhaps not. Unsettling as this uncertainty is sometimes, it is also a very exciting period in our lives, as a second youth, where choices are once again wide open.

My own instinctive feeling is that Rom's most valid contribution in the field of conservation is in the area of wildlife utilization and that this, if opportunity allows, should be his permanent parking lot. Small and trouble torn though it is, it is the Irula Cooperative which has probably been his most significant and lasting contribution to wildlife conservation in India. He has been able to demonstrate that preservation and exploitation can go hand in hand as a compatible team. His efforts in public education have paid off great dividends and as the 'Snake Man of India' he has played an important role; but it is not the main highway.

Rom's experiences in crocodile farming in New Guinea, Africa and elsewhere are very valid for developing countries, where the standard resource based industries bring only ecological havoc. The sustained use of crocodiles for their skins, simultaneously with an effective conservation programme, is an ideal management approach. And in my mind's eye, that's where he really fits in — in a croc infested swamp, his shirt disintegrating with sweat, and a small stubby pencil counting off crocodiles on a data sheet.

end page

Apart from the normal disadvantages that every woman married to a naturalist experiences, such as the fact that reptiles are always more interesting and important than me, I consider that I did a clever thing in marrying Rom. Initially the adjustments, especially the financial ones, and change of lifestyle, proved difficult though my parents and Doris helped in many different ways. But things got easier as we went along, and the consultancies in reptile management which FAO offered Rom made it possible to extend our house, build a small summer cottage in Kodaikanal, and feed two voracious sons.

I have never been too happy handling snakes but my interest in reptiles grew apace and fortunately. we turned out to be one of those rare couples who can work together non-violently. Soon I was steeped to the ears in Rom's work and we thought up, developed and worked on many things together as a team. I made it very clear from the start that he was to credit every success to me, and failure to himself, and this proved to be a good contract.

Life is interesting. Something new is always happening and our environment is a multi-faceted, stimulating one. Right now, for instance, the Croc Bank is buzzing. Jeff Lang, his assistant Simon Wakefield and

Croc Bank Manager Harry, are weighing and measuring crocodile egg shells in one corner, while Mike Ewert, the freshwater turtle expert, is trying to hatch flap-shell turtle eggs in the other. Mike is helping us upgrade our freshwater turtle breeding programme and training Chandini Menon to look after it. Also prowling around the office and lab looking for a place to sit, are Jack and Susanna Frazier, currently in India on a tortoise survey. At the Irula Cooperative, venom extraction is in progress and Dravidamani and Shyamala are weighing last week's venoms. Also at the co-op is frogman P Shekar who is doing a study, for Government, on the diet of frogs. The Irula have kept him supplied with specimens, and the most interesting one was a bull frog with a saw-scaled viper in its stomach.

Further down, eight Irula women are busy at work preparing nursery bags for their recently begun tree planting project. Nearby, Rom holds forth to three doctors from Bihar about crocodile farming. And at my office, three Irula come in to report a saw-scaled viper bite (not serious); Rajendran of BEEP says he has no bus money for tomorrow's school visits, Munuswamy drops in to say there's no cyclostyling paper left for *Hamadryad*, and my ten year old typewriter gets mysteriously locked.

Sometimes we feel we have spread ourselves out too thin — reptiles, public education, venoms, Irula, trees, films — and that we have been a little over ambitious. But having set things in motion it is impossible to stop, or even slow down, because it is the overall momentum which makes each separate project effective.

Glossary

Andha saamp — *blind snake.*
Ayyo sami — *Oh, God!*
Babul — *the thorny* Acacia *tree.*
Beedie — *thin, strong smelling cigarette made from tobacco leaf using no paper or filter.*
Chillum — *pottery, stone or metal pipe used for smoking marijuana.*
Dorai — *master.*
Ganja — *marijuana.*
Goli — *pill.*
Kum-kum — *red powder used in Hindu religious rites.*
Lungi — *an extended waist cloth worn mostly by men; it does slip off at times but a very comfortable garment.*
Nag Panchmi — *Hindu festival dedicated to the cobra.*
Pambukaran — *snake man.*
Patti — *small village.*
Phoorsi — *saw-scalled viper.*
Puthu balli — *a species of gecko.*
Rasagollas — *milk sweets, speciality of Bengal.*
Seri — *okay.*
Sholas — *general term in the south for evergreen forests.*
Suratai — *saw-scaled viper.*
Tamasha — *drama.*
Thambis — *younger brother, but also generally used, in friendship and camaraderie*
Toddy — *palm wine*
Veshti — *a garment, shorter version of lungi.*
Yaanai — *elephant.*

MORE ABOUT PENGUINS

THE LONELY TIGER

Hugh Allen

Ever since he was old enough to use a catapult, Hugh Allen dreamed of hunting big game. When he decided to settle down in India, a country he had been hospitalized in during WWII, his dreams were finally fulfilled.....

In the gripping true life stories in this book, the author recounts his encounters with man-eating tigers, love-sick tigresses, laughing leopards, killer boars and deadly snakes.

'One of the best books on tigers and hunting I've read'—*Stephen Alter*